The Dangers of Alternative Ways to Healing

ELLEL MINISTRIES
THE TRUTH & FREEDOM SERIES

The Dangers of Alternative Ways to Healing

How to Avoid New Age Deceptions

David Cross
and
John Berry

Sovereign World

Sovereign World Ltd
PO Box 784
Ellel
Lancaster
LA1 9DA
England

www.sovereignworld.com

Unless otherwise stated, all Scripture quotations are taken from the Good News Bible
published by The Bible Societies / Collins © American Bible Society.

Other versions used are:

NIV – The Holy Bible, New International Version. Copyright © 1973, 1978, 1984 by
International Bible Society. Used by permission.

NAS – New American Standard Bible ®. Copyright © 1960, 1962, 1963, 1968, 1971, 1972,
1973, 1975, 1977, 1995 by The Lockman Foundation. Used by permission.

LITV – The Literal Translation of the Holy Bible. Copyright © 1976–2000 by Jay P. Green,
Sr. Used by permission of the copyright holder.

KJV – King James Version of the Bible. Crown copyright.

NKJV – New King James Version. Copyright © 1983, 1992 by Thomas Nelson, Inc.

NLT – The Holy Bible, New Living Translation. Copyright 1996, 2004. Used by permission
of Tyndale House Publishers, Inc., Wheaton, Illinois 60189. All rights reserved.

ISBN 978 1 85240 537 3

The publishers aim to produce books which will help to extend and build up the Kingdom
of God. We do not necessarily agree with every view expressed by the authors, or with
every interpretation of Scripture expressed. We expect readers to make their own judgment
in the light of their understanding of God's Word and in an attitude of Christian love and
fellowship.

Cover design by ThirteenFour Design
Typeset by **documen**, www.documen.co.uk
Printed in the United Kingdom

Contents

Introduction

Many people seem disillusioned with modern medicine. There is a growing trend, when looking for an answer to life's problems, to experiment with alternative ways of healing, very often based on ancient philosophies and religious practices. Despite amazing scientific advances in medication and treatment, which have brought such wonderful relief to the sick, there is a growing view that modern drugs don't quite get to the root of the problem. In fact many people feel that the side effects of prescribed drugs can often seem to make matters worse.

Our bodies consist of much more than just flesh and bones. There is also an unseen part of us that needs restoration, but even the best of doctors and prescriptions don't really meet these deeper issues. This need for healing of the whole body, soul, and spirit is nothing new. From the beginning of mankind's existence, philosophers have sought an answer to this combination of our physical and spiritual needs. A word frequently used these days is the quest for a *holistic* approach to healing, recognizing the needs of the *whole* of our being.

Actually this approach fits remarkably well with the teaching of Jesus, who makes it very clear that mankind has deep spiritual needs which affect the whole of the body, both emotionally and physically. Unfortunately many people don't see Jesus as the foundational answer to any disorder in their lives.

In this book we shall be proclaiming that faith in Jesus is the best way of complementing the usually excellent treatment given in mainstream, science-based medical practice. However, for many people there is clearly something very attractive in the antiquity or the mysticism behind the countless alternative or complementary remedies being offered these days. Many of these methods are described as bringing healing to body, mind, and spirit, but are they safe ways to seek restoration for our spiritual well-being?

Near to where we live, several high-street premises have appeared in recent years advocating, in particular, ancient Chinese remedies which claim to restore balance and health to every part of the body. On television, in magazine articles, and even in the doctor's surgery alternative medical treatments and relaxation techniques are apparently growing in recognition and credibility. It is often claimed that these drug-free therapies are not only effective, but intrinsically more natural and therefore less harmful.

Recently, at Ellel Ministries Glyndley Manor, we were speaking to a lady about the frequent use of these therapies by herself and her family. She became upset as we suggested that she might take a fresh look at the safety of these methods, from a Biblical perspective. As we talked, she suddenly declared quite forcibly that since the Royal Family of the United Kingdom clearly considered alternative medical practice effective and safe, who were we to disagree? We felt it wise to postpone the discussion for another time!

Despite this viewpoint, Christians need to ask a very serious question. Are there unseen side effects with some alternative remedies? Is it possible that many of these procedures, whilst perhaps avoiding chemical intrusion into the body, could be permitting spiritual intrusion? Although there may be apparent relief from unwanted symptoms, is it possible that spiritual bondage is being stored up, only to be experienced at some time in the future? We will take the view that this is exactly what can happen, albeit unrecognized by both the patient and the therapist. We will look at different types of alternative diagnosis, medication, therapy, and exercise (including yoga and martial arts), some of which are now becoming part of mainstream health programs and even children's school curriculums.

This book has not been written to attack those practicing or participating in alternative remedies. It is intended to raise awareness of the fact that we all live in a spiritually challenging world where, according to the teaching of Jesus, the only safe solution to our spiritual needs is through Himself. Unfortunately, there can even be deceptive ways of spiritual healing that come with a "Christian" label and we will look at how to discern what is truly coming from Jesus and what is not. If this book increases debate on this subject of alternative remedies, we shall be pleased. If it brings freedom to some who have got caught in spiritual bondage, we shall be delighted. Throughout the book, all the names of those who have received prayer have been changed in order to maintain confidentiality. Chapter 9 gives suggestions for how you can pray about these issues where they may have affected your own personal life.

May the Lord continue to give us all more of His wisdom in this important subject.

CHAPTER 1

Understanding the Alternatives

Pathways to health

Good health is a universal desire in mankind. However, the pathways of healing are very many, both in procedure and effectiveness. For the purpose of this book, we are considering healing to be *the restoration of order and peace in our bodies*. For any person looking for healing, the basic process is essentially the same, irrespective of the type of therapy or medication. First seek a diagnosis for the cause of the problem, then consider the treatments being offered, and finally make a choice which route to take.

This choice of which pathway to follow for restoration of the whole person is very important, sometimes even a matter of life and death. The Bible acknowledges this choice and encourages us to look for God's best way. Unfortunately mankind has a tendency to believe that he knows best.

> *The LORD said to his people, "Stand at the crossroads and look. Ask for the ancient paths and where the best road is. Walk in it, and you will live in peace."*
> *But they said, "No, we will not!"*
>
> (Jeremiah 6:16)

In diagnosing sickness, it is not very popular these days to talk about sin. For the man carried to Jesus on a stretcher (in Luke 5), the forgiveness of his sin led to the remarkable healing of his paralysis. It seemed that the spiritual condition of the man's heart was affecting the physical condition of his body. The Bible makes it clear that it is mankind's sin in this world, both corporate and personal, which has caused the spiritual and physical disorder which we see around us.

Whilst ignoring the sin issue, many of today's alternative healing procedures claim to diagnose spiritual imbalance in the body as the cause of sickness. Sometimes instruments such as pendulums are used to determine the "aura" or spiritual field around a person's body. The Bible calls it "divination" and forbids God's people from using such procedures.

> *Don't sacrifice your children in the fires on your altars; and don't let your people practice divination or look for omens or use spells.*

(Deuteronomy 18:10)

In some parts of the world today, for example, it would not be uncommon for people to go to a local temple to seek help for sickness. Probably in response to payment, it would be normal for the temple priest to perform particular rituals in order to invite spiritual power to inhabit his own body and for this to be released into the sick person to effect their healing. The priest is acting as a medium. This practice is also forbidden for God's people.

> *There shall not be found among you ... one who casts a spell, or a medium, or a spiritist, or one who calls up the dead.*

(Deuteronomy 18:10–11 NAS)

We may see this as very far removed from practices that we would experience in the community where we live. However, in our hometown here in the UK there are places offering training and healing using similar techniques, for example in the practice of reiki. This treatment involves the channeling of spiritual energy through the practitioner and into the body of the patient. The therapist is acting as a medium. Christians seeking to walk in safety need to be aware of the many pathways to health available these days and also to be alert to the possible side effects of those remedies which may be invoking unseen and perhaps harmful forces.

We were looking at a prospectus the other day, for distance-learning courses from a reputable college in the north of England. One course was for the study of life-coaching skills, written by a New Age therapist, apparently described in a national newspaper as one of the new gurus who have got inside our minds to fill society's spiritual void. The same college was also running diploma courses on Personal Wellness, written by another therapist, specializing in esoteric energy, feng shui, and reiki. I wonder if the college authorities have given any thought as to whether the teaching is safe for their students, from a spiritual perspective.

We live in times when there is a deep spiritual hunger in the lives of many people throughout the world. We intrinsically recognize that healing of the body is more effective when there is understanding of the needs of the whole person – body, soul, and spirit. There are many safe therapies and lifestyles, complementary to mainstream medical practice, which aid the God-given pathway of healing in our bodies. However, Jesus says very clearly that His Kingdom is the only true answer when we have a need of spiritual restoration. We just need to be careful to avoid the false pathways and the dangerous minefields of the enemy!

Happy are those who know they are spiritually poor;
the Kingdom of heaven belongs to them!

(Matthew 5:3)

To think about: Jesus says *He* is the way (John 14:6). What could be the consequence of following other spiritual pathways in our desire for healing?

Vivienne's story

Vivienne's father was the local doctor in her hometown and he practiced homeopathy as a holistic alternative to mainstream medicine. Whenever his children were sick he would prescribe homeopathic medication and it seemed very effective; in fact Vivienne saw the homeopathic pills as almost miraculous. As she grew up, Vivienne was very attracted towards many alternative therapies, but at the age of twenty she became a Christian and began to feel uncomfortable about many of the things she had experienced in childhood. In particular, she felt that God was asking her to stop using the homeopathic treatment, even though her parents became upset with the new choices that she was making.

At church, she began to hear about Christian healing and was surprised to find that she experienced extraordinarily strong feelings of contempt and unbelief over the whole idea of God bringing miraculous restoration into people's lives. One day she was talking to her pastor about her experience of homeopathy as a child, and he suggested that it would be good to seek God's release from any effects that this holistic treatment had had on her life. She agreed and, during the prayer time, she was astounded to find herself speaking out in a very sneering and mocking way to those praying for her. She described later that it was as if something inside her was shouting that homeopathy was the only true miraculous healing!

She confessed to God the deep dependence that her family had placed upon homeopathic medication and asked Him to release her from any side effects of spiritual bondage. Despite some further moments of very dark thoughts and words of unbelief, she soon experienced a powerful deliverance and a clear sense of freedom from an unclean spirit that had apparently gained a very strong hold over her thinking. From that time, she found herself with a completely different view towards the healing ministry of Jesus. Vivienne described to us recently just how big a change that prayer time had brought in her life.

We will look later in this book at the practice and roots of homeopathy and try to understand why it was able to have such a strong effect in Vivienne's life. We will be exploring many different types of diagnosis, medication, therapy, and exercise which might have unwanted side effects on those seeking health and well-being.

To think about: Have I put too much trust in a particular therapy or remedy in preference to seeking Jesus for the help that I need?

Definitions

What do we mean by "alternative ways of healing"? A number of different words are frequently used, in a somewhat random way, to refer to medical treatment which generally lies outside the boundaries of what has historically been seen as mainstream medicine, particularly in Western culture. Having said that, the National Health Service in the United Kingdom, for example, is increasingly embracing treatments that, a few years ago, would have been regarded as quackery. Terms such as "complementary," "natural," "holistic," "Eastern," and "traditional" appear frequently to describe treatments that purport to provide an alternative pathway to health, avoiding or complementing medical practice based on the use of mainstream drugs and surgical procedures.

Many medical commentators would describe mainstream medicine as that which is quantifiable and repeatable, whereas alternative treatments appear much more random in both their ability to bring healing and also the degree of restoration experienced by the patient. By such definitions, healing through Christian prayer must also be seen as alternative, as it complements and sometimes replaces mainstream medicine. When we see God heal, it is miraculous, supernatural, and life-changing, but it is not quantifiable or repeatable through our own effort or wisdom. Christians believe that God knows what is needed and when it is needed. Seeking His healing is strongly encouraged throughout the Bible, but the results, however welcome, are always beyond our control!

The woman in the Bible with the problem of hemorrhaging was only too pleased to eventually discover an alternative solution to her twelve-year search for medical help, when she received a wonderful supernatural healing by Jesus.

There was a woman who had suffered terribly from severe bleeding for twelve years, even though she had been treated by many doctors. She had spent all her money, but instead of getting better she got worse all the time. She had heard about Jesus, so she came in the crowd behind him.

(Mark 5:25–27)

As with the teaching of Jesus, many alternative treatments recognize the link between the physical and spiritual condition of mankind. However, the procedures for diagnosis and remedy are completely different. Only Jesus declares that the basic problem is the separation of man from his Maker through disobedience, and that the only complete solution for restoration is through a response to the good news which He brings.

The Spirit of the Lord is upon me,
*   because he has chosen me to bring good news to the poor.*
He has sent me to proclaim liberty to the captives
*   and recovery of sight to the blind;*
to set free the oppressed.

(Luke 4:18)

To think about: Jesus offers an alternative or complementary way of deep healing, alongside the many benefits of medical science. How does He want me to respond to this offer?

If a therapy works, surely it's worth trying

This book is not written to determine whether particular alternative medical procedures appear effective or not. Our purpose is to explore the important issue of the spiritual consequence of such treatments and whether this can bring more harm than good to the body. In fact you could conclude that, if an alternative remedy seems to work, it is even more important to be sure that the relieving of a physical problem is not at the expense of creating a spiritual one. Jesus says that this world is currently being ruled by a spiritual being who seeks to intervene in the life of mankind. One of the names of this spiritual ruler is Satan. Only Jesus, who is completely without sin, has been able to walk this earth without ever being gripped by any of this ruler's power.

> *I cannot talk with you much longer, because the ruler of this world is coming. He has no power over me.*
>
> (John 14:30)

Clearly, Christians believe that the "alternative" or "complementary" healing ministry of Jesus, where His spiritual authority is fully in place, will only bring good results, both seen and unseen. But we must ask a question when considering many other alternative practices: Does Satan, the adversary of God and the enemy of men's souls, have an opportunity to establish something of *his* authority and power through the people and procedures being used in such practices? For some alternative remedies, the answer seems to be a very obvious *yes*. For others we may need to explore a little more deeply, bearing in mind that the predominant character of Satan is that he is a deceiver.

Today's challenge

The world, and its spiritual ruler, are bombarding us with supposed answers to man's quest for well-being. Take a look in your local bookstore at the shelf marked "Healing" (or something similar), and you will be likely to find titles and phrases such as:

Life Coaching, Detox Regimes, Chakra Healing, Herbal Cleansing, Essential Oils, Taoist Secrets of Life, The Power of Kabbalah, Out of Body Experiences, How to Harness Animal Knowledge, The Power of the Ancestral Mind, A Zen Approach to Life, Spiritual Healing, Positive Energies, Cosmic Ordering, Essential Tantra, Enneagram for the Spirit, Soul Therapy, A Guide to Visualization, Crystal Medicine, A Tarot Package, The Art of Yoga, Keeping Young with Tai Chi, Pilates for Everyone, Magnetic Therapy, Facial Reflexology, Numerology, A Medium's Guide to the Spiritual World, Color Healing, The Ascended Masters and the Spiritual Path, True Shiatsu, Eurhythmy, Zen Sexuality, The Way of the Spiritual Warrior and Martial Arts, Treatment with Hopi Candles, Learning Qigong, Medical Hypnosis, Gemstone Reflexology ...

... and indeed hundreds more alternatives!

Confused? The good news is that Jesus fully understands the spiritual realms, both the good and the bad, and we can entrust ourselves to His wisdom and His safe pathway for our restoration. We do not need to have expertise in all the therapies on this bewildering list, but it is important to have sufficient understanding in order to be able to avoid, and help others avoid, the spiritual pitfalls of many of these practices, which may trip us up through ignorance.

To think about: The spiritual realms are beyond our full understanding, but nothing is beyond the understanding of Jesus. Does that comfort me?

Increasing credibility

Maybe you feel that all this is still far removed from your experience of medical treatment, but increasingly many of these practices are being accepted by national regulatory bodies. Here in the United Kingdom, NICE (the National Institute for Health and Clinical Excellence) recently endorsed acupuncture and spinal manipulation as being fit for use within the UK National Health Service, whilst admitting uncertainty in the process and the effectiveness of the treatments. What regulatory body is considering the spiritual implications of particular treatments? Would NICE endorse witchcraft if they concluded that it apparently relieved symptoms for some people?

An interesting announcement appeared recently in the UK press by the General Regulatory Council for Complementary Therapies (GRCCT), saying that it was pleased to announce that practitioners of crystal healing were now able to be part of a national register, joining those involved with aromatherapy, energy therapy, massage, neuro-skeletal realignment therapy, reiki, and reflexology, representing more than 50,000 therapists. The GRCCT explained that the registration process operated in a similar way to the system used by the UK Nursing and Midwifery Council.

In this announcement, there was an implicit alignment of the credibility of the GRCCT, a body that is happily advocating the spiritual potency of gems and crystals, with that of the Nursing and Midwifery Council. We find it hard to believe that the latter organization would be happy with such a comparison.

We are beginning to see a new approach towards alternative treatments even from some in the mainstream medical world. It can be summarized as follows: *We may not know how it works, but if it sometimes works, let's include it in the procedures that we offer to patients.* Many governments around the world declare that they are very keen on health and safety issues these days, but who has done a risk assessment on the spiritual aspects of these alternative therapies which are increasingly being condoned by government authorities?

To think about: Where do we turn to find out what is spiritually safe? Jesus says we can learn from Him (Matthew 11:29).

The side effects

If you get medicine from the pharmacy there's usually an accompanying leaflet that explains all the possible side effects of the chemicals contained within the medication being sold. We are given the opportunity to consider these side effects and make a choice as to whether we take the medicine. Some, for example, might make us drowsy, while alleviating the pain for which we want relief. If we are involved in work which requires a high level of concentration, we may decide to look for another treatment rather than finding ourselves chemically controlled in ways that could cause harm.

These are physical or sometimes emotional side effects. But what about spiritual side effects? Is it possible that certain treatments and therapies, while apparently bringing some relief to our condition, are actually affecting the spiritual condition of our bodies in ways that are not directly seen but still put us in a place of harmful spiritual control? It is our intention to draw attention to these spiritual side effects because the treatments being discussed in this book do not come with a leaflet listing this possible unseen source of harm.

The extent of vulnerability to the chemical side effects of a prescribed drug depends on the physical and emotional constitution and condition of the patient. Spiritual side effects can similarly depend on the spiritual condition of the patient. For example, it appeared that Vivienne was particularly vulnerable to spiritual powers of darkness operating through homeopathy, at least in part, because of the lack of spiritual protection from her father in that area.

To think about: In what ways have my family been involved with occult healing practices which might have left me particularly vulnerable?

The way we are made

The Bible is very clear that we are, at the same time, both spiritual and physical beings. There is a part of us that can be seen and a part that cannot, a part constrained by time and a part existing in eternity, a part that is physically born and a part that needs to be spiritually born if we are to fully experience abundant life.

> *That which is born of the flesh is flesh; and that which is born of the Spirit is spirit.*
>
> (John 3:6 NAS)

The place where the physical and the spiritual parts of us meet is the soul, where thinking, feeling, and decision-making exist. We are designed by God to have a human body, a human soul, and a human spirit. Unfortunately these can all be damaged. The good news is that Jesus brings restoration for every part where there is a lack of wholeness or liberty.

> *May the God who gives us peace make you holy in every way and keep your whole being – spirit, soul, and body – free from every fault at the coming of our Lord Jesus Christ.*
>
> (1 Thessalonians 5:23)

Many alternative healing practices recognize the need for *wholeness*, physically, emotionally, and spiritually. Only Jesus teaches us the need, and provides the way, for true *holiness*. This need and this way are found with God's plumb line of truth and not through a pendulum of divination.

There is a spiritual enemy

As well as the world we see around us, there is a spiritual realm, unseen but very important for the well-being of our lives. Our spiritual condition depends on what spiritually controls our lives, just as our physical condition is dependent on the control of the physical world around us. Our bodies quickly suffer if we are trapped in cold, wet, hostile conditions. Spiritual hostility can be just as harmful. This, of course, is the very reason that Jesus came, to offer us freedom from what is spiritually harmful, and to give us a place of well-being where *He* is in control.

> *The Son of God appeared for this very reason, to destroy what the Devil had done.*
>
> (1 John 3:8b)

Satan is indeed the ruler of this spiritually hostile world. He was handed this rule by man's rebellion against God and seeks to gain or retain as much spiritual authority as possible through taking advantage of man's continued disobedience towards God. Satan gets the upper hand whenever we follow his ways rather than God's ways. Paul, the apostle, was only too aware of this principle and he was careful to keep right with God, particularly with respect to the issue of forgiveness.

> *When you forgive people for what they have done, I forgive them too. For when I forgive – if indeed I need to forgive anything – I do it in Christ's*

presence because of you, in order to keep Satan from getting the upper hand over us; for we know what his plans are.

(2 Corinthians 2:10–11)

We will look in more detail at the tactics of this enemy later in the book. In the meantime it is sufficient to remember that he can get the upper hand of spiritual authority wherever our lives are out of line with what God says is right. Satan empowers his authority using unclean spirits. It will be important to understand how such spiritual powers can get a foothold in our lives, particularly in the area of healing methods which are not God's way.

Summary

Nobody questions the importance of checking out the side effects of prescribed drugs in mainstream medical practice, but what about the spiritual side effects of alternative remedies which frequently advocate the need for a holistic approach to treatment? It is certainly not helpful to exaggerate the problem, but we do need to make careful choices in this spiritually dangerous world.

Listen! I am sending you out just like sheep to a pack of wolves. You must be as cautious as snakes and as gentle as doves.

(Matthew 10:16)

We have spiritual as well as physical needs in the healing of our bodies. The spiritual realms can have a significant effect on our lives in both good and bad ways. For a Christian, the safe way to health is to ensure that every remedy in which we participate is clearly consistent with the authority of Jesus.

The scientific advance in medical treatment has been amazing and very effective in improving our lives, but where a remedy seeks to bring spiritual as well as physical change to our bodies, we need to be sure that we are on a safe path. In the next chapter we will look at a little of the history of man's quest for healing.

CHAPTER 2

The Age-old Search for Healing

Sickness is not a new problem

One of the frequent things that children say is "I feel sick," meaning that something feels wrong with the inside of their bodies. This feeling affects every one of us at some time or other, and in many different ways. You may hear someone who has witnessed a traumatic event, or been involved in a particularly unpleasant relationship, say "It made me sick," meaning more an emotional feeling than a stomach problem. The word "heartache" refers to pain deep within our bodies, in a place that can certainly be felt but never seen, even under X-ray! Let's remember that sickness can affect every part of us: our body, our soul, and our human spirit.

We won't be surprised to find that people have felt sick from the earliest of times. We read in the account of the Fall in Genesis that pain would be a universal part of the human experience. God tells Eve,

> *With pain you will give birth to children.*

(Genesis 3:16 NIV)

Now let's look at a little history in sections defined by both time and location.

The prehistoric world

There is evidence of how people were treated when they were sick, stretching right back into prehistory. We know that people had problems in the body in very ancient times, as shown in prehistoric cave paintings in various parts of the world. The Paleolithic period from about 20,000 years ago has provided us with evidence of elementary surgery. In some places trephined skulls have been discovered. Trephining is the practice of drilling holes in the skull of living human adults (who go on living afterwards), possibly in an attempt to release pressure or even evil spirits. The practice suggests that human beings were exploring basic medical principles from the earliest of times.

Use was also made of herbal remedies, many of the same plants being used today in the pharmaceutical industry. However, there is also evidence of strong links between a clinical approach to medicine and a spiritual or religious element, particularly in the role of the shaman, the ancient medicine man. He features in prehistoric paintings and archaeology as well as in more recent, though still ancient, cultures. An early example of this was found in a burial site in Israel dating from about 9500 BC where the individual appears to have been a "medicine woman," buried with the tools of her trade.

To think about: People from the earliest of times have been aware of the spiritual side to our problems. The Bible has been saying the same ever since it was written!

And He said to the man, Because you have listened to the voice of your wife, and have eaten of the tree about which I commanded you, saying, You shall not eat from it, the ground shall be cursed because of you; you shall eat of it in sorrow all the days of your life.

(Genesis 3:17 LITV)

The ancient Egyptians and the Middle East

When we look at the Egyptian period, dating from about
3000 BC to around 400 BC, there is written evidence on preserved
papyri of a more systematic approach to healthcare. We know
that a simple system of public health was developed in Egyptian
culture to try and minimize infection and disease. Documents
containing details of medical diagnosis and prescription have
been found, notably in the Edwin Smith Papyrus, which is a
document from 1600 BC (written when the Israelites were in
Egypt) containing accounts of medical practice back to 2600 BC.
This papyrus concentrates on surgery and details particular
ways of dealing with a variety of types of bodily damage,
developed from observations made of men wounded on the
battlefield.

In contrast, the Ebers Papyrus of about 1550 BC, which
preserves for us the largest record of ancient Egyptian medicine
known (the scroll is about 20 meters long), contains some
700 "magical" formulae and remedies. Medical matters were
dealt with through spiritual rituals, mainly using incantations
and spells, showing a general belief that sickness was not just a
physical issue.

Whilst the Egyptians were developing their medical
expertise, the Babylonians were also seeking to find out what
makes a person sick and how to deal with it. A physician named
Esagil-kin-apli wrote a work called *The Complete Diagnostic
Handbook* in about 1050 BC (the Davidic period in Jewish history),
which contained lists of diseases, and how to treat them with
pills, creams, and bandages. Again the diagnosis was based on
close observations made of sick people, just as we would do
today. Interestingly, in this work, the non-physical element of
the sickness was not included in these diagnoses.

To think about: Whilst the ancestors of Moses were
praying for God to heal them, their neighbors in Egypt were
going to "doctors" who did basic surgery but also used spells

in their treatments. God's name in the Old Testament, Yahweh Rophi (the LORD who heals), meant that He was always available to heal the sickness of His people.

He said, "If you will obey me completely by doing what I consider right and by keeping my commands, I will not punish you with any of the diseases that I brought on the Egyptians. I am the LORD, the one who heals you."

(Exodus 15:26)

Asian medicine

When we look further east, we find a different stream of thinking about medical issues. There is evidence that an early civilization in what is now Pakistan knew something of both medicine and dentistry. Drilled teeth from around 9000 BC have been discovered there! A scholarly system of medicine was developed in about 400 BC and written down in a text called *The Science of Living*, or *Ayurveda* (taken from the Sanskrit word *ayus* meaning "longevity"). This was based on ancient sacred texts from India written between 1500 BC and 1000 BC called the Vedas, and included contemporary herbal practices used in medical treatment together with many other religious ideas, some coming from Buddhism and Jainism.

The basis for this system of treatment was composed of both empirical (what they observed) and spiritual concepts. Indeed, mysticism and Hindu ritual were very much a part of the Vedic thinking. It is also worth noting that the Brahmins (Hindu priests and rulers) encouraged good personal hygiene in order to prevent disease, which is still a very good policy in today's world!

Chinese medicine was also being developed into a systematic form during this period, originating in the teachings of Taoism, founded in the seventh century BC by a man named Lao-zi. *Tao* means "the way," and Taoism focuses on a spiritual pathway for exploring ideas of health, nature, longevity, effortless action, and spontaneity. It also has links into other Chinese disciplines including martial arts, traditional Chinese medicine, and qigong (a meditative technique for apparently improving the flow of spiritual energy through the body). The belief in spiritual forces was at the heart of traditional medical practices, and this became the dominant feature of Chinese medicine.

The foundational text of Chinese medicine is the *Yellow Emperor's Inner Canon*, which is composed of two books: the *Suwen* (Basic Questions) which dealt with theoretical Chinese medicine, and the *Lingshu* (Divine Pivot) which dealt with acupuncture. This work was written between the fifth and first century BC (after the exile of Israel to Babylon). It put forward the concepts of *yin*, *yang*, and *chi* as being spiritual life forces in the universe which affect human well-being and which can be manipulated within the human body. *Yin* is said to be the negative feminine force and *yang* is the positive masculine force. Illness was believed to result from the *yin* and *yang* being out of balance. These concepts are foundational to many of the alternative remedies in use today.

To think about: Most of the Old Testament had been written before the appearance of the main book on which traditional Chinese medical practice is based.

Ancient Greek and Roman medicine

The Greeks, in their search for knowledge, inevitably included the desire to understand the human body. The first medical school was established in about 700 BC at Cnidus. Hippocrates, 300 years later, developed the Greek medical practices into a teaching regime in his hospital on Cos, thought to be where the Hippocratic Oath originated. This oath, which has been amended over the centuries, was a promise to maintain an ethical standard in all medical practice. Although not generally adopted by qualifying doctors nowadays, the original oath, pronounced in the name of the supposed healing deities of the time, contained high ideals of behavior such as a refusal to ever take a life, including through abortion.

The Greeks' interest in observation drove them, in trying to find out how things worked, to put more emphasis on scientific reasons rather than supernatural ones. The philosopher Aristotle was fervent in his observations of nature and in developing the discipline of biology. He also decided that the rational soul was located in the heart, not the brain. His successors pursued biological and botanical studies in their quest for an understanding of life, and a hundred years later a medical school at Alexandria was founded, where physicians explored the nervous system and relocated the soul back into the brain!

Early Roman understanding was founded on the belief that healing was the domain of the supernatural and magical, and was best reserved for the lower levels of humanity, which is how they regarded their slaves. However, as Greek culture spread over the Roman Empire this view gradually changed, and the Romans used evidence-based diagnosis coupled with the Greek approach to treatment and began building hospitals for their soldiers, as well as their slaves.

To think about: By looking harder at God's creation, people learnt more about themselves. Many of them also recognized that there must a Creator behind it all, although they did not "know" Him personally.

Old Testament medicine

There are only a few specific references to the activities of medical practitioners in the Old Testament, but there is some mention of ways of treating disease, and the existence of physicians is at least recorded. These were men who practiced both magic and elementary herbalism. In Genesis we read of the physicians being called by Joseph to embalm his father Jacob around 1850 BC.

Then Joseph fell on his father's face, and wept over him, and kissed him. And Joseph commanded his servants the physicians to embalm his father. So the physicians embalmed Israel. Forty days were required for him, for such are the days required for those who are embalmed; and the Egyptians mourned for him seventy days.

(Genesis 50:1–3 NKJV)

In the second book of Chronicles we are told of Asa's mistake in consulting physicians instead of trusting God, which led to his death around 870 BC.

In the thirty-ninth year of his reign Asa was afflicted with a disease in his feet. Though his disease was severe, even in his illness he did not seek help from the LORD, but only from the physicians. Then in the forty-first year of his reign Asa died and rested with his fathers. They buried him in the tomb that he had cut out for himself in the City of David. They laid him on a bier covered with spices and various blended perfumes, and they made a huge fire in his honor.

(2 Chronicles 16:12–14 NIV)

Jeremiah, in the period after the Exile, acknowledges the existence of physicians in Gilead, a place renowned for its healing spices and herbs, and the Apocryphal book of Sirach has a long passage commending the ministry of the physician, written in the time between the Testaments (Sirach 38:1–15). The Old Testament word for "physician" has its roots in the concept of a cure, not just the treatment of sickness.

Is there no balm in Gilead?
  Is there no physician there?
Why then is there no healing
  for the wound of my people?   (Jeremiah 8:22 NIV)

Chapters 13 to 15 of Leviticus have detailed instructions for dealing with skin infections, sometimes referred to as "leprosy," and these methods were clinical procedures (based on actual observation and treatment of disease rather than experimentation or theory) together with spiritual rituals. The story of Naaman (2 Kings 5) shows that disease in the land of Canaan was a normal part of human experience and that it was also believed to be treatable.

Although little is known about how physicians operated, it is clear that both medical and herbal practices were used for physical ailments and that there was also a strong underlying awareness of the spiritual dimension to sickness within the Old Testament world.

To think about: God is the oldest "holistic" Healer in history. When Jesus came to the earth, He showed how true restoration – in body, soul, and spirit – could be found.

From Christ to the Age of Enlightenment (eighteenth and nineteenth century)

In AD 129 a Greek boy named Galen was born in the Turkish city of Pergamum. In his teens he began to study medicine at a temple dedicated to the Greek god of medicine, Asclepius. He researched Aristotelian ideas, and at the age of nineteen inherited considerable funds which enabled him to travel the Mediterranean world in search of medical knowledge. In AD 157 he returned to Pergamum where he took up a position as physician to gladiators (a very prestigious position), which enabled him to study the effects of trauma and sports injuries at first hand. In AD 168 he moved to Rome where, as physician to the Emperor Marcus Aurelius, he was able to promote the Greek practices of medicine extensively. He wrote more medical texts than any other person in the ancient world, and his writings formed the foundation for Western medicine for more than a thousand years.

In the early part of the fourth century AD the Roman Empire had adopted Christianity as its official religion, and the Church became the preserver of medical understanding. The way of dealing with sickness was based primarily on the Western principles established by the Greeks. From this time, right through the medieval period, the care of the sick was largely handled by Church institutions such as the monastic orders. The Benedictine Order, for example, saw their whole ministry as caring for the sick. The methods employed by the Church were based on Hippocratic medical practice, but treatment included consideration of the spiritual issues. Unfortunately the general view of suffering – that it was sent by God as a direct punishment for personal sin – made a concerted attempt at healing rather difficult to embrace! As a consequence, many believers embarked on pilgrimages or regimes of penance as a means of securing personal healing.

Alongside the basic Hippocratic approach to medicine during the Middle Ages, there was a continuing belief in folk medicine. Even the clerics frequently employed herbal remedies, often embracing superstitious rather than scientific thinking. Magic still flourished as a common pathway to healing, and local apothecaries extensively used the supposed supernatural qualities of herbal remedies in their treatment.

However, towards the end of the first millennium there were developments in medical training, notably in the Arab world, where pharmacy and chemistry were established alongside medicine as scientific studies, and practicing physicians were expected to have been formally trained. The tenth-century caliph of Baghdad required all medical practitioners to have taken an examination before they were licensed!

Also in this century, medical establishments developed apart from clerical control, such as the school of medicine established in Salerno, Italy, which was also open to female practitioners. Here medical texts from the Byzantine and classical era of the Greeks and also from Arabic medical writings were translated into European languages, and were combined to become a standard basis of instruction for all medical practice for the next few hundred years. Developments in surgery also spread in Western Europe during the Middle Ages, adding to the growing understanding of how the body works and what was needed for its healing.

In Western Europe from the sixteenth to the nineteenth century there were increasing advances in medical understanding, including a new and fairly accurate theory of the nervous system, along with developments in surgery. Medicines still remained largely the same as they had been for many hundreds of years, based on opium and quinine together with local herbal concoctions.

However, the Industrial Revolution of the nineteenth century saw major advances in both medical research and development and a resulting significant change in medical practice.

To think about: It's not surprising that when God worked healing miracles, people often thought it was magic, given the superstition of the age. The same happened when Simon Magus saw the Holy Spirit at work in Samaria (Acts 8). We need revelation to recognize the true hand of God.

From the Age of Enlightenment to the present day

At the beginning of the so-called Age of Enlightenment, particularly in Western culture, there were many new technological advances. Industrialization allowed equipment to be developed and made to a standard never before achievable. Research progressed into the nature of disease and many new products appeared to treat illnesses. As a result, medical practice moved away, almost completely, from the earlier approach of providing both physical and spiritual treatment, in favor of a purely clinical approach to health and healing.

Rapid developments of vaccines, antibiotics such as penicillin, and the progress in medical techniques resulted in great leaps forward in dealing with sickness, disease, and surgical needs. The concept of holistic health – considering unseen spiritual needs – was sidelined in favor of the evidence-based approach. Religious or spiritual causes for ill health were largely rejected and everything was viewed as relevant only if it could be determined by the five senses. The Age of Reason was a time when people wanted to deal in hard facts, not spiritual revelation. A God-centered view of life was becoming "old-fashioned."

At one level, this was a good thing, in that most medical practitioners no longer dabbled in what had often been dubious religious or superstitious practices, but now concentrated solely on the scientific aspects of health. Western medicine therefore came to provide a generally safe environment for treatment of many clinical issues, free from unhelpful mystical intrusion. At another level, the more fundamental theological or philosophical issues behind medical matters were mostly overlooked. Medical practice was increasingly able to treat the *bodily aches* successfully but not the *heartaches*. The new approach was a bit like being able to analyze a cake into its constituent parts, but choosing not to consider why the baker made it a particular color or shape in the first place.

To think about: Considering that most of the medical advances today have come from close observation of God's creation, little is said, in medical institutions, about the Creator's own views as to why things have gone wrong!

So why the interest in alternative medicine today?

Many people today feel that the drugs-and-surgery approach is not necessarily the most effective answer to their lack of health. To just keep taking tablets does not seem to address the real state of sickness in the heart of man. There is a feeling that there must be a better, more rounded approach to meet our true needs. Therapies and treatments which appear to offer help for the parts of our lives that mainstream remedies can't reach are therefore attractive, especially when there have been disappointments with conventional medicine. In addition, people are feeling increasingly devalued as they sometimes consider themselves reduced to a statistic on a hospital efficiency program. There is a heart cry being expressed by many: "I want someone to understand *me* and give *me* time!"

As a consequence, the wheel of the story of medicine seems to be turning full circle and those who are offering holistic remedies are once again being sought. This is just as it was in the early days of medicine, when mankind demonstrated an awareness of his need for healing to every part of his being. The problem is that once we mix the physical repair of the body with remedies for spiritual restoration, we need to be very sure that the therapist is on safe spiritual ground.

Summary

From the earliest times mankind was aware that sickness was both a physical and spiritual issue. As civilization developed, so the understanding of the human body increased. In Eastern culture there has generally been a degree of partnership between the physical and the spiritual approaches, in trying to find healing for the whole person. In Western culture the situation gradually separated into two systems, the mainstream evidence-based approach standing apart from those remedies considered to be the alternative practices, which looked more to the spiritual roots of sickness.

However, there has been, more recently, a renewed interest in alternative ways of healing even by those practicing mainstream medicine. But this presents a problem: there is now a blurring of the boundaries between the scientific and the spiritual approaches. In the same way that we need to be able to trust that sufficient clinical investigation has been carried out on the chemical safety of mainstream medicine, so we also need to satisfy ourselves that the basis for a holistic treatment is one of spiritual safety. Let's now consider a little more why we are so drawn to alternative ways of healing.

CHAPTER 3

What's the Attraction?

Green grass

We have a saying in English: "The grass is always greener on the other side of the fence," meaning that if something is a little beyond what is made available, it can somehow seem much more attractive. If there is a flock of sheep in a field of grass, you can guarantee that at least one of them will try to get its head through the fence to sample the delights of the field next door! When things are not going too well in our own situation, someone else's solution somehow seems so much better, irrespective of whether it really is effective or whether we truly know the facts of their circumstances.

After the time of Solomon, a new ungodly king appeared on the throne of the Northern Kingdom of Israel. His name was Jeroboam. He felt that by diverting his people away from worshipping the Lord in Jerusalem, he could keep them more fully under his own control. He built new altars and shrines which became more attractive than the way of worship established over the two previous generations. He made golden calves and proclaimed:

Here are your gods, O Israel, who brought you up out of Egypt.

(1 Kings 12:28b NIV)

37

As a result the nation of Israel became even more divided, and it never reunited under the true worship of Yahweh. The grass appeared greener in this new field and the attractions of false religion lured the people away.

In our society today there is much dissatisfaction with the status quo. As we write this book, much of the world is in the midst of a serious economic crisis and many governments have faced the possibility of public unrest and overthrow from within the nation. The old structures no longer seem to work, and alternatives are being sought on many fronts – economic systems, ecological systems, and inevitably, spiritual systems. The temptation is to try out new alternatives without really being aware of what they involve or what truth, *or lies*, might be behind them. This certainly applies to the world of health and healing.

A New Age beyond the age of Christianity?

Although the phrase is less used now than it was a few decades ago, "New Age" philosophy has been a very important factor in the recent growth of alternative therapies in Western culture. From the period of the so-called Age of Enlightenment in the eighteenth century, through the theosophical societies in the next, and to the "flower power" of the 1960s, there has been an increasing belief that the age of the narrow spiritual pathway of Biblical Christianity is outdated and restrictive. As the New Age movement grew during the 1970s in the West, there was a widespread search for mystical experience, almost without boundaries, using anything that seemed to work. Spiritual gurus, diverse meditation techniques, and hallucinatory drugs all played an important part in the quest for a new meaning to life and the desire for new ways to health and well-being.

The New Age is not a clearly defined movement with structure and leadership, but an international network of groups and individuals exploring religious and philosophical ideas in a quest for spiritual knowledge, enlightenment, and improvement. It specifically denies the Biblical authority of Jesus and is, in fact, a form of Gnosticism, one of the deceptive movements that troubled the early Church. Common New Age beliefs include pantheism (all that exists is god), reincarnation (rebirth in another form after death), *karma* (accumulation of the effect of a person's deeds in life, leading to reward or punishment), auras (energy fields around the body), and personal transformation through mystical experience, ultimately with the hope of a new world order.

A typical New Age practitioner might, for example, explore channeling (acting as medium to the spirit world), the healing energy of crystals, meditation and music to attain new levels of consciousness, and divination using astrology, Tarot cards, or a pendulum. In particular, a significant part of New Age understanding is that there is a need for a holistic (body, mind, and spirit) approach to human health, both in diagnosis and in treatment. Most of the alternative therapies and treatments described in this book could be included under the general heading of "New Age techniques."

To think about: Many people believe that Christianity is outdated. However, Paul saw Jesus as the answer for every age:

> *Unto him be glory in the church by Christ Jesus throughout all ages, world without end. Amen.*

> (Ephesians 3:21 KJV)

Dissatisfied customers

Today many Christian believers are dissatisfied with the depth of spirituality offered by the Church. A prominent church leader recently declared a deep personal unmet hunger. He expressed a conviction that there must be so much more to the spiritual life than he had yet discovered, despite more than two decades of his own Christian walk and ministry.

Whilst this leader was searching for a deeper spirituality within the Christian Church, he also discovered that many people shared a similar desire, albeit without a commitment to the Gospel of Christ. In fact there is a worldwide search for deeper spiritual fulfillment and the New Age movement has attracted a vast number of ordinary people into its ranks as a consequence. People have become fascinated with the spiritual realms. This is not really surprising when we recognize that we were made by God to find spiritual harmony with our Creator. Paul recognizes this when he writes:

> *May the God who gives us peace make you holy in every way and keep your whole being – spirit, soul, and body – free from every fault at the coming of our Lord Jesus Christ.*

(1 Thessalonians 5:23)

Men and women are designed to have a covenant relationship with God, who is Spirit. This fellowship is the true doorway to wholeness and freedom in every part of our being.

In a recent Christian-sponsored research project in the UK it was observed that there is a growing demand for some sort of alternative approach to life, for new answers to old questions. The dissatisfaction with life has led to a renewed emphasis on spirituality. In the research, true "wealth" was seen by many to be as much spiritual as material. People were exploring an alternative scale of values in order to restore meaning to their lives. In fact, 27% of the people surveyed claimed to have successfully changed their spiritual life and a further 20% declared that they would like to do so.

To think about: If this is a time of growing spiritual dissatisfaction, is it surprising that people are particularly vulnerable to the deceptive ways of the enemy?

There must be a better alternative

The problem we have is that those who are seeking change in their spiritual lives are often turning to alternative therapies and practices, without necessarily being aware of the roots of such remedies and the possible dangers for those, even Christians, who engage in them. We have a friend called Simon, who suffers from both physical and mental health problems. He has been prescribed many strong conventional medicines but, for a while, chose to reject them in favor of alternative remedies, because he came to the conclusion that the side effects of the mainstream medication were far more harmful than the side effects of using naturopathic remedies and even cannabis to relieve his pain.

A first response to this could well be, "He's probably right!" However, we need to consider this a little further. About a hundred years ago, Benedict Lust, the so-called father of naturopathy in the United States, described the body in spiritual terms and declared our well-being to be reliant upon the cosmic forces of man's nature. Naturopathy, which quite reasonably seeks to minimize the use of prescription drugs and surgery, sounds attractively natural. However, it actually covers a wide range of alternative therapies and medication, homeopathy being one of the most common. We suggested to Simon that he needed to look at the spiritual as well as the chemical side effects of the medication he was choosing.

There has been considerable research and discussion over many years into the physical and emotional consequences of using cannabis. This drug comes in many forms and with varying degrees of strength. In the stronger varieties it can, without doubt, have a hallucinatory effect on the body. It seems very clear from the accounts given by those who have experienced hallucinatory "trips" that there is a breaking down of the spiritual integrity of the body during some of these episodes. In other words, through certain drugs, the order and wholeness of the spirit and soul can be seriously affected by the chemical trauma on the body. These drugs include cannabis and even some prescribed treatments which have been used to treat psychosis.

Lasting inner spiritual brokenness is very likely to be a consequence for some people who have used drugs like cannabis. Who is telling people like Simon about such possible side effects? We must be free to make our own choices, but surely these should be from a position of understanding the true consequences of these decisions.

To think about: Not every remedy that seems to work is necessarily good for us. The apostle Paul wrote that although all things may be *permissible*, not everything is *beneficial* (1 Corinthians 10:23).

Old is apparently good

A further reason for this rise of interest in alternative remedies is the belief that much mainstream medicine involves procedures and medication that have been more recently developed and therefore inadequately tested by the evaluation of time. People feel that products are sometimes marketed seemingly without sufficient trials, and indeed occasionally treatments do go very wrong. These mistakes, of course, always make headline news.

Where healthcare is state funded, lack of government finance can result in extended waiting times for treatment, together with increasingly stretched and stressed medical staff. Cost-cutting can mean research is put on hold, so that the expected new treatments are not always available, and the medicines themselves are sometimes too expensive to be prescribed, except in acute cases. In some countries, target-driven healthcare, pursuing satisfactory statistics rather than satisfied patients, has led to frustration in many areas.

People who already had doubts about the ability of modern medicine to produce the required healing find themselves turning away from mainstream practice, as they are tired of waiting for something that seems increasingly unable to meet their needs.

We live in a world where our rights, including those connected with healthcare, are promoted as absolute and necessarily to be demanded. The inevitable result of this distorted view is that people are increasingly frustrated by any failure to meet their expectations, and feel the need to find a place of blame. Newspapers fuel the trend as they report the stories of those who have experienced modern treatments that have gone wrong, often with graphic pictures to illustrate their point. The occasional horror stories from mainstream medical practice inevitably do the world of alternative therapy a powerful favor. When your neighbor reports how bad such-and-such a treatment was for them, you are unlikely to go seeking the same thing for yourself!

By contrast, alternative therapies apparently offer remedies that have been tried and tested for generations. It can seem sensible to try a healing practice which has a long pedigree rather than wait for a new discovery which may or may not work. If a treatment originated 3,000 years ago and is said to have worked ever since, it inevitably becomes an attractive alternative to a modern remedy. Again, the reports of friends whose symptoms seem to have been dealt with by alternative therapies can be influential in encouraging people to try the same for themselves. Unfortunately, symptom control is often incorrectly seen as a treatment of the hidden cause. Weeds need to be pulled out at the roots if there is to be a lasting solution. If there is some digging to do in our lives, it is best to look for a safe gardener.

To think about: God has been healing people since the beginning of the world. His nature as the Healer has not changed. He is not a modern remedy that is unproven.

The search for holistic well-being

There is a direct connection between the spiritual journey that many embark on and their search for healing through alternative therapies. The basic philosophy behind these therapies is that the body, mind, and spirit are all parts of the whole person, a view which the Bible agrees with, although body, *soul*, and spirit might be better terms. In order for healing to be effective, or indeed for any lasting improvement in well-being, the whole person has to be taken into account. Regular exercise can be very beneficial to every part of our being, but practices such as yoga, for example, have at their roots a fundamental spiritual belief. This may be very appealing to those wanting to explore their inner self, but the all-important question is: *What spiritual powers are being unearthed at the roots of these investigations?*

This growing holistic approach is gaining "official" endorsement in many countries. As mentioned earlier, in the UK the National Health Service (NHS) is now embracing and promoting many alternative therapies. In fact it now publishes a directory of such practices and practitioners. The NHS Directory website states:

> *The NHS Directory of Complementary and Alternative Practi-*
> *tioners [is] compiled and managed only for use by NHS healthcare*
> *professionals by the NHS Trusts Association, the leading profes-*
> *sional association for primary care in the UK ... The intention of*
> *The NHS Directory is to provide dedicated easy access listings of all*
> *practitioners, who by a process of self selection have put themselves*
> *forward to work either directly in NHS practices or from their own*
> *practice on a referral basis.*

The NHS in the UK is thus allowing complementary and alternative practitioners to have access to patients via their doctor, with apparently very little NHS screening. Therefore individuals open to a holistic approach to healing, although starting with conventional medical contacts, can easily find themselves directed towards alternative practitioners. In recent years in the UK it has therefore become much easier, and increasingly more acceptable, for any member of the public to explore alternative therapies. When the long waiting lists for mainstream medical treatment seem to delay the process of getting help, every alternative that is more accessible becomes very attractive.

To think about: Who is checking out the therapists to whom people are being referred for treatment, in order to determine the basis and the safety of their practice?

Easy access

An added attraction for those looking to alternative therapies is that the practitioners are increasingly available on the high street. In many towns throughout Europe, for example, where traditional businesses have folded, the premises are surprisingly often taken over by alternative therapy centers. The attraction of easy access is a huge one in our quick-fix society. A person in search of something to make them feel better can drop into an alternative therapy shop, often seven days a week, and receive immediate attention from a person who seems genuinely interested in them. They can often get a referral to an alternative practitioner for treatment within hours, or at most a few days, together with a bottle of "natural" medication from off the shelf.

When, particularly in the UK at the present time, this is compared with the increasing difficulty of obtaining appointments to see a doctor at the local surgery, followed by a long wait to see consultants, have tests, receive diagnosis and then treatment, all of which can take months, the drop-in practitioner on the high street can become very appealing. The local doctor's surgery will likely have alternative therapy leaflets and posters on display, so looking for help elsewhere is positively encouraged. As for seeking help through the local church, few people even begin to consider that there could be a source of healing there!

To think about: What a shame that Christian healing seems inaccessible to so many in our local communities, because churches are restricted in opening times and frequently offer no clear advice on the healing ministry of Jesus.

Meeting my need

Most people are fairly pragmatic. They will use something if it appears to work. A researcher recently looked at a number of alternative outlets on the high street of an English West Country town. His conclusion was that there was much more evidence of healing in those practices than he had found in most Christian churches in the area. For many people, the alternative therapies on the high street seem to meet their needs. But what is that need?

On offer from such establishments is usually something greatly needed by each of us: personal, caring contact. This may be in the form of words that express real concern, or touch that brings much-needed comfort. Massage, for example, is a common aspect of many alternative treatments. In contrast to the often rather cold clinical contact received in mainstream healthcare, where frequently the medical worker wears gloves for health and safety reasons, the alternative therapists invariably make very personal contact with their clients. Touch matters to all of us but can be particularly poignant for a lonely or needy person.

However, there is a problem. The Bible frequently reminds us that when hands are used to bring about impartation of something from one person to another, there can be an important spiritual dynamic. Of course this can be completely harmless in the touch that expresses friendship or shared feelings. For Christians, touch can be an opportunity for powerfully declaring the impartation of the Holy Spirit's gifting to and through the Body of Christ.

> *Do not neglect the spiritual gift that is in you, which was given to you when the prophets spoke and the elders laid their hands on you.*
>
> (1 Timothy 4:14)

If, however, the touching of hands is intended, through the particular philosophy of an alternative treatment, to impart some form of healing power, there is an important question to ask: What spiritual authority, operating in and through the therapist, is behind the intended power to heal? There is much talk these days of the need for medical staff to take great care not to transfer harmful bacteria through unwashed hands, but do we recognize that unclean spiritual powers can be transferred by the use of hands that are not operating under the authority of Jesus? The beliefs and practices of the therapist are very important when considering the spiritual safety of their touch on our body. Our hunger for contact can be an opening for the deceptive ways of the enemy, if we are careless in the need for discernment.

Following the fashions of the world

Another part of the attraction of alternative therapies is their trendiness. Fashion can play an important part in bringing people into using certain remedies or exercises. Tai chi evening classes at the church hall, yoga instruction on our smart phones, aromatherapy beauty products in high street stores, Indian head massage at the hairdresser, naturopathic infusions from the chemist ... the list is endless in our likely encounters with the world of fashionable alternative lifestyles.

If everyone is doing it, why should we swim against the current? Following fashion is essentially a walk along a lifestyle pathway determined by the world, and quite possibly the ruler of this world. Probably one of the most important spiritual gifts needed in the Body of Christ in these end days is the gift of discernment, in order to differentiate, by the prompting of the Holy Spirit, the spiritual basis of all that we encounter in this complex world. When uncertain as to how to respond to each day's new experiences, little children look to Mum or Dad for direction. We can always do that with our Heavenly Father.

As well as the growing fashion to explore alternative remedies, there is considerable interest in Eastern philosophies to direct our business lives and even in the ordering of our homes. Feng shui has become a commonly used principle for making choices of interior design. The concept appears regularly in magazines, suggesting that this ancient principle will bring increased harmony to a home and its occupants. How many people really understand that feng shui comes from a Taoist belief promoting the need to align things in order to permit the best flow of spiritual energy? Put more bluntly, it is a way of trying to appease the territorial spiritual powers in a locality to bring well-being to our homes and our lives. If feng shui is seriously adopted as part of a pathway to healing for ourselves and our environment, we need to be clear what power is being invited into our lives. It is *not* the power of the Holy Spirit.

We are blessed these days with a huge variety of wonderful international cuisine, both from the supermarket and in restaurants. Few people think twice about eating out in a place serving Asian food, but how many take notice of the decoration – the Hindu or Buddhist religious artifacts around the restaurant? What gods do the staff worship and what spiritual covering is there over these places? Is the food offered to an idol before being placed on our table, as would be the custom in many of these cultural traditions? The food that we eat is a critical part of the choices that we make to ensure a healthy way of life. We need to be aware not just of harmful chemical additives but also of the possibility of spiritual contamination. Those preparing the food have no intention of doing us harm, but there is a need for awareness that we can, and we suggest should, ask the Lord to cleanse all that He has given for us to eat.

Sometimes we are asked why it is not just as effective to ask God to cleanse an alternative treatment before receiving therapy. If saying grace works for food, why not for an occult therapy? The fact is that there is a very important difference. Food is essential to our lives and is provided by God for the well-being of our bodies through the fruitfulness of the earth. It may get spiritually defiled on the journey from the source to our mouths, but we can ask God to restore the condition of His gift to us through prayer. However, alternative therapies which originate in spiritual darkness are not a gift from God but a counterfeit from the enemy. God will never want to bless or cleanse what has not come from Him. He simply wants us to turn away.

When we say grace before a meal, we have a precious opportunity for not just thanking God for the provision of food, but also for forgiving those who have, even unconsciously, added spiritual defilement to what God has provided. As we forgive them, we can ask God to release the food from all that would be spiritually harmful to us, whatever the source. We happily wash our hands before taking food; praying before we eat is simply an opportunity to spiritually "wash" the food as well! We remember our Christian friend Harry, who was from a Chinese family, finding himself experiencing a quite unexpected deliverance at a Chinese restaurant when he remembered, a little late in the meal, to ask God to cleanse the food he was eating.

You shall have no other gods before me.
You shall not make for yourself an idol in the form of anything in heaven
above or on the earth beneath or in the waters below. You shall not bow
down to them or worship them ...

(Exodus 20:3–5 NIV)

The issue of dependence

It is not unusual to find that where people have become interested in alternative therapies, this interest has become a fascination or even an obsession. When a belief begins to take control over our lives, it is very important to be sure of the spiritual authority behind that belief. When people get hooked on drugs they crave the next fix. It can seem surprisingly similar with the intensity of search that some people pursue in their quest for personal health. We were looking recently at a book about aromatherapy, in which the author happily stated that she lived and breathed the practice. There is nothing wrong with strong convictions, but if we regard something as a life-giver we need to recognize the significant level of control of our lives that we have handed over to the treatment in question.

There is an enemy of souls who gains spiritual authority when we become dependent on things and people that are not what God has commanded for our lives. Physical pain can make us desperate. Anything that will bring relief seems worth a try, but it remains important to be honest with ourselves as to where we have put our faith. There can be a repetitive nature to some treatments that should cause us to consider what is really happening. When we find ourselves seeming to become over-dependent on the next visit to a particular therapist, it is time to check with Jesus, who wants us to find relief in safe places, with safe people, and with safe medication. Of course mainstream medical practice will often rightly require many sessions of treatment to reach the desired conclusion, but it is important to be aware of the issue of wrong dependence.

To think about: Bearing in mind the deceptive tactics of the enemy, do we need to be a little more careful in the way that we conduct our lives in order to keep ourselves as clean as possible in this spiritually fallen world?

Spiritual naivety

We were reminded earlier that when the apostle Paul was writing to the church in Corinth, he was concerned to help them keep alert to the plans and devices that Satan uses against followers of Jesus. He did not want Satan to be given the opportunity to get the upper hand (a place of spiritual authority) in their lives, not wishing these concerns to be a place of fear but rather a place of understanding in order to avoid harm as they went about their earthly lives (2 Corinthians 2:10–11).

Jesus has always had, and always will have, the upper hand over Satan. When we follow Him and His ways in all that we do, we too can be in the place of spiritual authority over the powers of darkness in our lives. Many Christians choose to belittle the tactics of the enemy, claiming that he should not be given too much credit for the disorder in this world. Of course, our focus should never be on Satan's domain, but Jesus taught His disciples to regularly seek the Father's direction to avoid the pitfalls of the ruler of this world.

> *And do not lead us into temptation, but deliver us from the evil, for Yours is the kingdom and the power and the glory to the ages. Amen.*
>
> (Matthew 6:13 LITV)

Indeed, Jesus wants us to be as "wise as serpents," and as "harmless as doves" (Matthew 10:16 KJV).

Summary

There is an increasing desire among many Christians for a deeper spirituality in their lives. The same is true for many in the world who have a different faith or even none. The search for holistic healing corresponds with this desire to find real answers to troubled lives. Unfortunately there is a lack of clear teaching on the true healing and deliverance ministry of Jesus, even in the Church. Very often, concerns with drug-based medicine, dissatisfaction with mainstream medical treatments due to long waiting lists, impersonal practitioners, highly priced medicines, and changing fashions have given rise to an ever-growing interest in alternative therapies.

Increased availability and respectability of alternative treatments, together with the desire for more personal care, have all added to this interest. Many of the alternative therapies, medication, and exercise regimes seem to improve symptoms for a significant number of users. The problem for those seeking spiritual safety is, however, not *whether* a therapy appears to work, but *why* it works. What belief lies at the root of the treatment? Christians are encouraged in the Bible not to remain spiritually naive but to seek increasing wisdom from their Heavenly Father, in order to enjoy the true well-being intended by their Creator.

CHAPTER 4

Understanding the Roots

Religions and philosophies

Behind all alternative remedies there are beliefs and philosophies that may have been newly embraced in New Age thinking but are actually not new ideas. In fact they are rooted in historical religions and philosophies which have sometimes been repackaged for today's world. When we explore these ancient religions we find that there is a complex overlap of beliefs and traditions. We certainly don't need to be experts in world religions in order to understand the foundations of many alternative remedies, but it's worth looking at a brief summary of the relevant beliefs within a few of these traditions.

Taoism means the study of "the way." This belief system reveres many deities and holds ancestors in particular respect. The human body is believed to find strength and well-being when it is correctly aligned with the universal cosmic life force, *chi*. There are opposing spiritual forces called *yin* and *yang*, which need to be brought into balance to allow a harmonious flow of energy through everything.

Taoism can be an influence, for example, in acupuncture, shiatsu, martial arts, homeopathy, reflexology, chi kung (or qigong), feng shui, and reiki.

Hinduism is based on the authority of sacred texts called the Vedas and promotes the existence of an enduring soul that migrates from one body to another at death (reincarnation) and also the law of *karma*, which determines one's destiny both in this life and the next. Although worship of particular gods is not essential, most Hindus are devoted followers of one of the principal gods: Shiva, Vishnu, or Shakti. The ultimate goal of all Hindus is release (*moksha*) from the cycle of rebirth (*samsara*) in order to be united with the supreme deity.

Hinduism can be an influence, for example, in yoga, Pilates, meditation techniques, color therapy, chakra healing, and massage.

Buddhism is largely based on the teachings of an Indian ascetic called the Buddha (the awakened one) who apparently discovered and taught the *dhamma* (the truth). It promotes a pathway of spiritual development apparently leading to enlightenment, happiness, and an insight into the true nature of life, using various practices, particularly meditation. Although rejecting the authority of the Vedas and the need to worship particular deities, this path includes beliefs similar to those of Hinduism such as *karma* and reincarnation, eventually achieving *nirvana*, the ultimate escape from the cycle of suffering and rebirth.

Buddhism can be an influence, for example, in meditation, yoga, Pilates, and hypnosis.

Pantheism is the belief that everything that exists is part of a universal god. All of nature is apparently a part of god or at least a universal spiritual entity or intelligence. It is associated with a number of other religious beliefs such as Hinduism and Taoism. Pantheism lies at the root of much New Age thinking, where the quest for this spiritual energy or life force, in order to find both enlightenment and well-being, is a common theme.

Pantheism can be an influence, for example, in naturopathy, crystal therapy, aromatherapy, some herbal remedies, and chiropractic.

Is there a life force?

When we looked earlier at a brief history of medicine throughout the ages, it was apparent that there has always been a philosophical argument as to whether mankind is simply a mechanical being, given life through chemical reactions, or whether there is an unseen spiritual driving force that sustains life. With the coming of a more mechanistic or clinical approach to human health over the last few centuries, the belief that there is a need for spiritual input and well-being has waned.

However, the Bible clearly teaches that we are made in the image of God, who is Spirit, and that we are given both spiritual and physical life through His creative power. The human spirit imparted by God into each human being returns to God when we die.

> *Then shall the dust return to the earth as it was: and the spirit shall return unto God who gave it.*
>
> (Ecclesiastes 12:7 KJV)

Jesus tells us that we all experience a poverty of spirit in this life which happily is able to be restored when we seek to establish His Kingdom in our lives.

> *Happy are those who know they are spiritually poor;*
> *the Kingdom of heaven belongs to them!*
>
> (Matthew 5:3)

Yes, there is a life force, but for Christians this is not some impersonal spiritual energy that we need to tap into for our well-being, but the Creator God of the universe, revealed in His Son Jesus Christ and active in us through the Holy Spirit. Jesus says that He is not just the Way but also the Truth and the Life that each one of us desperately needs (John 14:6).

To think about: We are more than just a complex machine. We are made in the image of God. Surely He alone really knows our spiritual needs.

Challenging cultural tradition

We were talking recently to a young Chinese Christian man about acupuncture and commenting on the possible spiritual side effects. He seemed to get increasingly upset and clearly felt that we were undermining centuries of his family tradition. We were reminded that someone once told us that you frequently discover the idols in someone's life when you experience a particularly angry response to any challenge to a person's beliefs. As this young man became more and more hostile, he said, "This is deeply rooted in our tradition. Maybe the original belief in how it works no longer applies, but that's no reason to throw out something that we have relied upon for generations. We will find out how it works one day!"

We fully understand that our cultural traditions can be very important and are certainly not necessarily bad for us. We indeed have no right to undermine cultural values simply because they are different from our own. However, Christians have made a decision to participate in a new Kingdom, with a radical new culture that focuses on the teachings of Jesus. He challenged the traditions of His time when He walked on the earth, not to condemn but to show a fundamentally new way of life which would bring peace to troubled hearts. Traditional ways can be good or bad. It is important for Christians to be willing to see their national culture from God's viewpoint. We can arrogantly believe, in Western culture, that our traditions are in line with God's Kingdom. We would do well to look carefully at every cultural background that we represent and ask the question: "Is the way we seek healing in our culture the way Jesus does things in His Kingdom?"

Acupuncture is indeed very strongly rooted in the traditions of Chinese people. There are strong claims for its efficacy. Our question is this: If it does apparently work (at least sometimes), how does it work? Ancient, and indeed many modern, practitioners have said that the piercing of the skin with specifically located needles unblocks the critical spiritual pathways in the body and restores health. Other practitioners say that, though it is not at present clear how it works, there will eventually be a known scientific basis. God has indeed given mankind the ability to increasingly understand biological mechanisms. It is certainly possible that there is more to learn about acupuncture, but if a tradition that is thousands of years old has strongly stated that this therapy is based on powerful spiritual principles, we should at least be very cautious of who or what could be in spiritual control of the procedure. We will consider this in more detail later.

Where does the power to heal come from?

Typically in mainstream medicine, the process of healing is understood to be the result of quantifiable chemical or surgical intervention and procedures, alongside the body's remarkable ability to restore itself. In alternative therapies there is usually a reliance on the intervention of an unseen energy or spiritual power which is based on certain belief systems.

Christian healing can also be described in this way and can thus be regarded as an alternative or rather a complementary procedure to mainstream medicine. The Christian belief is that through the death of Jesus on the cross, God has opened up an opportunity for spiritual (and consequently physical) healing in a world which has been defiled and distorted by sin. Those seeking healing through Jesus Christ, alongside mainstream medical treatment, put themselves clearly under His spiritual authority. Whatever spiritual power God uses to bring healing is then entirely subject to the safety of that authority.

If, however, a spiritual power to heal is invoked in a particular therapy and this power is not based on a belief in Jesus Christ, there exists a serious doubt as to whose spiritual authority is controlling the healing process. From a Christian perspective, some healing practices would very obviously come under occult and ungodly spiritual authority. Yoga, for example, may provide attractive exercise therapy for various bodily dysfunctions, but the practice ultimately forms part of an Indian traditional belief system intended to bring spiritual unity with a supreme Hindu deity. It is very likely that any healing power experienced in the exercises will be subject to the spiritual authority of the Hindu beliefs and gods which are being acknowledged in the breathing, meditation, and bodily postures.

Some therapies may seem less clear as to where the spiritual power originates. Aromatherapy is often marketed as simply a way of enjoying nice oils and nice smells. However, for many practitioners of this therapy the power to restore health is based on a belief that plants contain an unseen energy that, if transferred to the human body, will bring healing to our being. No deities are invoked by name, but what is the source of this apparent spiritual energy or power? God has given us plants both to eat and to be a source of therapeutic chemicals, but He has not encouraged us to see plants as a means of spiritual restoration. If healing power is experienced through aromatherapy we must seriously question the spiritual authority being established. It is much more likely to be a false deity than the God and Father of Jesus Christ.

To think about: Who could be in control of healing remedies that purport to meet our spiritual needs but do not acknowledge Jesus as the only way to truly know our spiritual Father? Does it matter?

The source of spiritual restoration

Because of the way God made us, mankind has always known that he needs spiritual restoration. It has been variously described throughout history as a need for a life force, a vital force, or a personal spirituality that needs harmony, balance, or enlightenment. Whatever the terminology, the most important question is: *Where do we go to find this spiritual restoration?* Nearly all alternative therapies claim to have found the answer. The choice is ours, but it is wise to make this choice very carefully and very clearly. Pick-and-mix is a great idea when choosing candies but a dangerous idea when seeking spiritual well-being. It can be as harmful as drinking dirty water. The clean part may be fine, but the contaminated part does the damage.

This is why we have been looking at the religious or spiritual roots to the age-old quest for healing. Just because a therapy is old, it does not necessarily make it safe, just as it is not the age of water that makes it fit to drink but the purity of the source. Christians have made a very serious decision in their lives – that is, to believe that only Jesus Christ is the pure Way, the Truth, and the Life in man's journey towards spiritual enlightenment and restoration. This means, for Christians, that every other religious belief that denies the claims of Jesus is impure and will not meet the spiritual needs in man.

> *Jesus answered, "Those who drink this water will get thirsty again, but those who drink the water that I will give them will never be thirsty again. The water that I will give them will become in them a spring which will provide them with life-giving water and give them eternal life."*
>
> (John 4:13–14)

For example, the philosophy of Taoism provides some amazing and very ancient perspectives on the way men and women should live, but it will never provide the spiritual truth of Jesus that changes and heals lives. Water from a Taoist source will carry impurity. *Yin* and *yang*, the opposing spiritual powers that apparently need to be brought into balance to allow the free flow of *chi*, the universal life force, remain interesting concepts, but they are incompatible with the way that Jesus has taught us how to be born again of the Holy Spirit in order to find true life.

Who is the founder?

It is also very important to look at the beliefs of the person who founded any particular therapy. We frequently call such a person the "founding father" of the treatment or practice. Father figures carry significant influence on those who follow them. We need to be aware of the spiritual inheritance which comes from those who have established certain principles or paths of healing.

One example would be the founder of chiropractic. Many chiropractors today would consider themselves to be practicing clear science-based procedures in the manipulation of the spine to relieve distortion of the nerve connections to the various organs of the body. However, the techniques of chiropractic were seen very differently by the founder, Daniel David Palmer. Both he and his son believed that chiropractic treatment removed interference to the flow of "Innate Intelligence" in the human body. As a practicing spiritualist, D.D. Palmer considered the healing principles of chiropractic to have been given to him from "another world" and he saw himself as the spiritual father of all chiropractic treatment, apparently occupying a position similar to other religious founders including Christ, Mohammed, Mrs Eddy (of Christian Science), and Martin Luther. He referred to himself as the "fountainhead" of chiropractic in both its scientific and religious aspects.

The Palmer College of Chiropractic was begun by D.D. Palmer in 1897 in Davenport, Iowa. The college itself has often been referred to as being the "fountainhead" of chiropractic, a term which certainly seems to imply a spiritual source. We need to consider the spiritual purity of any fountainhead or source for what we believe and what we practice. The therapy of chiropractic may have come a long way since the days of D.D. Palmer, but have today's practitioners clearly acknowledged and even renounced their spiritual roots? The effect of spiritual inheritance is a significant Biblical principle, bringing blessing or cursing on families depending on the godliness or ungodliness of father figures whose lives have influenced the family lines.

Our fathers sinned, and are no more;
It is we who have borne their iniquities.

(Lamentations 5:7 NAS)

Most practitioners of healing therapies today, especially those with a Christian commitment, probably have no intention of walking in the spiritual footsteps of the founder. However, a defiled spiritual inheritance is not cleansed by simply walking away from the beliefs of the founder, but rather by confessing the sin and forgiving those who have allowed defilement into the source of the therapy. It is possible that, without recognizing the significance of the history of a particular method of treatment, many therapists may be operating under a spiritual inheritance which could be harmful both to themselves and to their clients.

To think about: The founder of any therapy introduced not just techniques but beliefs. For any particular remedy that we have experienced, do we agree with the beliefs of the founder?

Who is the practitioner and what else do they practice?

A Christian dance therapist recently wrote these comments to us:

> *I have indeed experienced and witnessed non-Christian influences in many alternative medical practices, some of which do not seem in themselves to have any offensive base. Osteopathy, for example, was invented by Andrew Still, the son of a Methodist minister in the USA, and yet I have had osteopathic treatment and at the same time received energy and chakra healing – without asking for it – and ignorantly thought it was harmless, simply because I didn't believe in it.*
>
> *After hearing teaching at Ellel Ministries recently, you will be glad to hear that when I needed recent osteopathic treatment I rebuked everything [the therapist] said about energies and chakras, bringing God into every minute of our conversation. I must say, she seemed very happy to get rid of me! My experiences would suggest that we should seek out a Christian therapist or at least someone who doesn't have an unclear esoteric background.*

Osteopathy (or osteopathic medicine) is essentially a manipulation therapy that seeks to correct abnormalities in the musculoskeletal structure of the body, mainly in the spine. This is usually in the belief that these defects can cause dysfunction in the body as a result of damage to nerve activity and fluid flow. There is a wide range, throughout the world, of training and treatment, from those practitioners that regard osteopathy as simply an extension to mainline medical practice, to others that see it as a truly holistic and alternative therapy, sometimes aligned with naturopathy. For many, there is no sense of any spiritual dimension to osteopathic treatment but, as the example above shows, we always need to check out the true beliefs of the practitioner.

Summary

The origins of a therapy are like plant roots that are underground and unseen, but they feed the plant with the nutrients that are needed for survival. If the roots reach down into contaminated water, the whole plant will be affected and poisoned.

Most alternative remedies are based on beliefs founded in ancient religions such as Taoism, Hinduism, and Buddhism. Many of the principles from these ancient beliefs have been adopted into New Age thinking and practices. The Bible encourages us to take seriously the spiritual inheritance affecting our lifestyles today. The founders of many alternative therapies had strong beliefs about the supernatural world and its involvement with healing. The concept of a universal life force or intelligence, which can be manipulated to bring healing through a multitude of techniques, is frequently at the root of the beliefs behind alternative medical practice. We should remember that the Holy Spirit is not an unseen force that can ever be manipulated!

The spiritual authority which rules over any alternative therapy, and therefore the spiritual safety of the remedy, are both dependent on the beliefs of the original founders, the beliefs of today's practitioners, and, not least, the faith of the patients receiving the treatment. Good fruit depends on both a good tree *and* good roots.

CHAPTER 5

A Closer Look at Alternative Diagnosis and Therapies

Checking out the side effects

In the next two chapters we are going to look at some specific examples of alternative diagnosis, therapy, medication, and exercise regimes, including martial arts. We are picking out examples that will give us an opportunity to look at the principles and the areas of concern which are typical of many other alternative treatments.

In the appendix of this book you will find a comprehensive list of many of the commonly found alternative practices. There is a short explanation of the treatment together with an indication as to why it could bring harmful spiritual side effects. Not all the side effects listed on the packaging of mainstream medicines, purchased at a pharmacy, affect everybody in the same way. It depends on the physical condition of the patient. In the same way not everyone will experience spiritual difficulties with the various treatments which are being considered in these chapters. It will depend very often on the spiritual vulnerability of the recipient. If, for example, there has been a history of previous occult practice in the life of an individual or in their family, there can be an added tendency for the spiritual darkness associated with these therapies to bring further bondage.

Diagnosis of the human body or the human spirit?

Doctors practicing mainstream medicine will usually carry out a detailed examination of a patient, in order to diagnose the root issue which is causing the symptoms. Through many checks and tests, they are evaluating the presenting symptoms and the malfunction of the various organs of the body to determine the particular disease which needs treatment. They are looking at the body as a machine that needs specific repair in the places of damage, through medicinal or surgical treatment. The doctor is evaluating your clinical condition.

If, however, you seek help at an establishment offering Chinese remedies, for example, it is likely that the most important aspect of the diagnosis will be examination of your tongue and pulse rate. Of course these can be very helpful indications of bodily dysfunction, but the therapist who is following traditional Chinese medicine is actually seeking to evaluate the balance of spiritual forces within the body (*yin* and *yang*) and the flow of the spiritual life force (*chi*) through energy channels (meridians) in the body. The traditional Chinese medical doctor is actually diagnosing your spiritual condition.

In a similar way, other alternative practitioners will seek to evaluate (or divine) a person's healing needs by checking their aura, the supposed energy fields surrounding the body, apparently related to emotional and spiritual well-being. Some practitioners might use Kirlian photography to produce an image of this energy field; some might use crystal therapy, placing stones on or around the body to diagnose and then treat energy imbalance; some might use color therapy to check the *chakras* (so-called energy centers) in the body; some might use radionics devices to check the apparent frequency of the body's energy output from, for example, pieces of the patient's hair. When assessing the safety of a particular treatment, it is important to register the questions asked during the preliminary consultations with a therapist. If these include questions about your star sign, for example, it is immediately clear that there is an occult basis to the diagnostic process.

"Radiesthesia" is another name given to the detection of this apparent spiritual radiation or aura around the body. In such diagnosis, the practitioner may hold rods or a pendulum over the client and watch the particular movements associated with certain parts of the body. The therapist is, in effect, inviting spiritual power to operate through both himself and the dowsing instrument, in order to divine the medical condition of the patient. Of course divination is strictly forbidden by the Bible (Deuteronomy 18:10), not least because the invitation of this unseen power can be an open door to intrusion from Satan's domain.

Let's take a look at applied kinesiology. This is not the same as kinesiology, which is the scientific study of human movement. Applied kinesiology was originated by a chiropractor in 1964 and is used as an alternative medical diagnosis for a number of disorders, including allergies. The procedure involves the assessment of muscle resistance, for example the response of the arm to being held down. This is supposed to correspond with the health of particular organs in the body. Although used by a significant number of chiropractors, there is virtually no scientific support for the procedure and it is seen by some practitioners to rely on the theory of meridians, in a similar way to reflexology. When we choose to put our faith in such practices, we need to recognize the danger of what we may be permitting to have control over our bodies.

To think about: When a particular therapist is assessing the cause of my sickness, is he or she using methods based on a proven scientific system or on a supernatural belief system?

What is being examined?

If, in a search for healing, you were to visit someone using the beliefs of Scientology, the therapy would be based on a system of ideas and practice called Dianetics. The diagnosis of your problem (called an "audit") would be through counseling with, probably, the use of an electropsychometer, an electrical device supposed to measure mental dysfunction (engrams) affecting your spiritual identity. This identity or life force is known as a "thetan," a spiritual entity which inhabits the body through a process similar to the Hindu belief of reincarnation. Needless to say, there is nothing remotely compatible here with the Bible's view of how sin has damaged our lives, both spiritually and physically, and how God brings restoration through belief in Jesus.

We need to be cautious with treatments using apparently scientific and sometimes sophisticated-looking equipment. The jargon used in advertising can be misleading and we can easily get the impression that if there is enough machinery or electronics involved, the diagnosis and treatment must be free of any spiritual side effects. Mora Therapy™, for example, uses high-tech electronic equipment, apparently to measure and then cancel out unbalanced energy patterns in the body which cause disorder. However, this treatment, according to some advertising literature, is effective essentially because it is a practice combined with the principles of acupuncture and homeopathy.

A visit to an iridologist would result in close examination of your eyes. The practitioner will study the colors and patterns of the iris in order to apparently determine the condition of the various organs of the body. The procedure was first promoted by a Hungarian physician in the nineteenth century and became better known through the work of an American chiropractor in the 1950s. Diagnostic charts showing a link between parts of the iris and parts of the body are similar to those used in reflexology where zones on the sole of the feet (or sometimes the hands and ears) are said to be linked to particular organs of the body by unseen pathways, or meridians. There is no scientific evidence for these pathways and no Biblical basis for their existence. Any faith we put in these practices is a choice to believe in spiritual powers outside the authority of Jesus and ultimately a choice to invite deception and darkness into the diagnosis of problems in our lives.

God uses a plumb line, not a pendulum

Discovering what is wrong with our lives is of course important. Mankind certainly has a spiritual problem and this is at the root of all sickness in the world. Through our breaking of covenant with God we have lost the intimate relationship with Him that is the source of the abundant life which He designed for every one of us to experience. The basic problem has always been sin, both corporate and personal, but *not one* of the diagnostic procedures used in alternative medical practice addresses this truth. There is much talk of the need to realign or rebalance the flow of the "vital force" needed for a healthy body, but no mention of the need to tackle sin.

The Bible does not recommend a pendulum to ascertain our spiritual condition, but God has given us the picture of a plumb line to help us understand how our lives can be out of line with His truth.

> *[The LORD] asked me, "Amos, what do you see?"*
>
> *"A plumb line," I answered.*
>
> *Then he said, "I am using it to show that my people are like a wall that is out of line. I will not change my mind again about punishing them."*
>
> (Amos 7:8)

These are serious words that God is speaking to His people through Amos. They are heading for disaster because of their refusal to follow God's instructions for the safety and well-being of their lives. They have decided that they know best! When a plumb line is held up alongside a wall under construction, there can be no doubt as to whether the wall has been built truly vertical. Walls which are out of line are very vulnerable to collapse. A plumb line lies perfectly vertical because of the *physical law* of gravity.

Whenever God's people are leading lives that are out of line with Him and likely to bring destruction upon themselves, it is very important that someone lifts up the truth of God's Word to allow His *spiritual laws* to show the straight line. Of course we have a choice to acknowledge or to ignore this line. God's intention through His plumb line is not to condemn us but to bring us to a place of confession and receiving His forgiveness. This is the basis for all true divine healing but not, unfortunately, the basis of any alternative therapies – except the "Jesus alternative."

To think about: What is likely to be the safest way of assessing my spiritual condition: comparing my life with God's plumb line of truth, or divination using a pendulum?

From diagnosis to treatment

Once the diagnosis has been carried out, it is time for the treatment. At the clinic for traditional Chinese medicine, you may be offered a variety of ways forward including acupuncture (applying needles to specific parts of the body), hot cupping (applying suction using small cups, similar to acupuncture), acupressure or shiatsu (applying specific pressure similar to acupuncture), electro-acupuncture (using electrical impulses), moxibustion (applying heat together with, or instead of, acupuncture), or buqi (non-touch vibration therapy).

We mentioned before that just recently and for the first time in its existence, NICE (the National Institute for Health and Clinical Excellence in the United Kingdom) recommended some complementary therapies for use in the National Health Service in England and Wales. The recommendation was particularly related to treating back pain with therapies such as spinal manipulation and acupuncture. Many medical experts immediately responded by saying that there was no evidence for such treatments being any more effective than a placebo. NICE admitted that it was still not completely clear how acupuncture worked, but they felt that the evidence showed that, on balance, patients did better with these therapies than with other less cost-effective procedures.

Let us say again that, in this book, our look at such complementary therapies is not so much exploring whether they work but rather whether there can be spiritual side effects which could be harmful. It seems that NICE is unwilling to consider that issue.

Acupuncture is an ancient Chinese procedure, probably going back some 5,000 years. It has been used for the treatment of many physical and emotional disorders, as well as for alleviating pain and inducing anesthesia during medical operations. The classic text of acupuncture theory and practice, the *Nei-ching*, makes it clear that the treatment is based on the Taoist dualism of *yin* and *yang*, and the need to bring balance to these opposing spiritual forces within the human body. The insertion of needles, or applying suction, heat, or pressure at specific locations of the body, is intended to bring balance and the free flow of the *chi* or life energy along unseen pathways or meridians. There is no known science to support the diagnosis or treatment of imbalance within energy pathways in the body.

We noticed recently the comments of a practitioner saying that oriental medicine cannot be separated from its philosophical underpinnings. If acupuncture works, how does it work? There are three possible answers: through an undiscovered scientific process; by a placebo effect; or lastly, through a spiritual power associated with the Taoist philosophical roots. Apart from the use of acupuncture in anesthesia, no reasonable scientific theories have been generally accepted. Some researchers on pain believe that acupuncture somehow sends signals to the brain which compete with or eliminate pain signals, or that puncturing the skin could help release endorphins or other body chemicals which can blunt or mask the pain. But what about the claims made by practitioners for healing of disorders throughout the body?

True or false healing?

Let's look at acupuncture from a spiritual viewpoint. If the procedure is essentially an invitation to an unseen and unknown healing power, is it possible that it is an unclean spirit that is blocking the pain sensation or providing a form of false healing? That was certainly the case for Tony, who felt the Lord convicting him that it had been wrong to seek healing for his addiction problems through acupuncture some years before we met him. As we prayed for Tony to be cleansed from any spiritual defilement from the treatment, he experienced clear deliverance each time we touched and anointed with oil the places where the needles had punctured the skin. For Tony there was no doubt that this pathway of healing through acupuncture had been a route of false healing which had hindered the true restoration that Jesus was bringing into his life.

One practitioner recently commented that acupuncture is most effective when the patient believes in and submits to the procedure. Believing in something is indeed an act of spiritual submission. If Jesus is not at the center of the belief, there is a real opportunity for the enemy to gain a foothold with unclean spirits. This possibility of demonic intrusion takes the whole issue of alternative healing beyond something that is merely unhelpful or ineffective to something that could do spiritual harm.

Paul warned the church in Corinth that careless practices which are, in effect, acts of spiritual submission, idolatry, or sacrifice can be an opening for the powers of darkness, even in the life of a Christian.

> But the things the nations sacrifice, "they sacrifice to demons, and not to God." But I do not want you to become sharers of demons.
>
> (1 Corinthians 10:20 LITV)

To think about: The need to repair spiritual disorder in the body is certainly recognized by Jesus, but His solution is not to manipulate forces along meridian lines but rather to establish His Kingdom in our hearts.

Some therapies seem so natural

We have previously taken a brief look at aromatherapy. Let's look a bit more closely. Perfumed oils, anointing oils, and soothing oils are all found in the Bible. Surely God has given these to mankind for his well-being. Very true! But what exactly are we asking for the oils to provide? Is it for something that will soothe the skin where there is soreness and something that will provide a wonderful scent when our senses need stimulating, or are we expecting more? The beliefs of many aromatherapists could be summarized as follows: Every living thing has a life force, energy, or soul. The life force of a plant is something that cannot be seen, but it is contained in the essential oil of the living plant. It is the energy from the life force of the plant which is introduced into a person by aromatherapy, each oil apparently having its own healing effect on certain parts of the body, including the mind.

If this is indeed the belief system of the therapist, we are entering a realm of spiritual invocation, well beyond the place that the Bible gives to the plant world in God's creation. We are touching into a pantheistic belief which says that our relationship with the spiritual life force in nature is the basis of our well-being. Use of plant oils is not wrong unless we use them in ways that do chemical harm to the body, use them with massage techniques that have a suspect spiritual basis, or put our trust in some supernatural property in the oil beyond what God intended.

Interestingly, one therapist commented recently that she considered aromatherapy to be a truly holistic treatment, and once again the observation was made that it was very important for the recipient to have confidence in the therapy when treating ailments. We surely need to be very careful where we put our trust when seeking healing. Faith, trust, and confidence are all acts of submission to a person, a practice, or a product. Our trust defines the spiritual authority over our lives. Thank God that faith in Jesus is completely safe.

The significance of touch

Massage is worth taking a moment to consider – it can be so pleasant! We recommend that every married couple should take the opportunity sometimes to massage each other's feet. It is just wonderful after a stressful day, and the pleasure of both giving and receiving can be very special. This sort of activity is entirely harmless. But unfortunately, massage in a wrong way can carry spiritual or even sexual "baggage" that can be very defiling. It is typical of the enemy's domain to seek to steal what God has meant for good. Reflexology is not simply a form of foot massage. Whether it is carried out by a therapist or a machine, it is a technique, once again, intended to use unseen pathways in the body to restore spiritual harmony. We have seen that belief in these meridians is a common foundation to many alternative treatments, generally coming from a Taoist or Buddhist background.

Other forms of massage, such as huna massage (an ancient Hawaiian technique), Thai massage (manipulating the so-called *sen* pathways in the body), zero balancing (a modern technique based on similar principles to acupressure), and cranial-sacral therapy (intended to identify and release energy blockages) all take massage treatment into the supposed realm of energy balance or similar beliefs about the spiritual condition of the body. Such practices are related to what is sometimes referred to as the "bioenergy" of the body. But "energy" is simply a word meaning the effect of *power*, and we need to be very careful as to what form of power is involved.

Are these therapies simply enhancing the chemical and electrical power of the body in the muscles and nerves or do these practices step into the spiritual realm? The language and beliefs expressed in most of these therapies clearly point to a spiritual basis. It is not too unusual these days for even a hairdresser to start providing Indian head massage, albeit uninvited, apparently seeking to unblock our energy channels, thus curing all sorts of problems – including baldness! However, touch and massage are not necessarily harmful. We just need to recognize that hands laid on us can be an opportunity for spiritual impartation and we need to be sure that we are in a safe environment.

A friend in France recently told us of the increasing popularity of a touch therapy called Haptonomy™. Started by a man from the Netherlands, this therapy, when frequently used during pregnancy, is intended to encourage emotional contact between the parents and the unborn child, through specific touch on the mother's abdomen. Acknowledgment and affirmation of an unborn child are very important for the well-being of the whole family and Haptonomy™ would seem to encourage this in a significant way. The only caution might be that it is worth noting that the spiritual openness of a growing fetus makes it particularly vulnerable to both good and bad environments. Amazingly, the Bible tells us that John the Baptist leapt in his mother's womb when he became aware of the presence of Jesus in the womb of Mary (Luke 1:41). It is very important to ensure the spiritual safety of the words and actions of any therapy which is intended to make connection with an unborn child.

The Bible is full of examples of hands being laid on people to bring healing. Jesus imparted healing many times in this way. There is clearly spiritual significance in the use of hands, so it is vital that we are comfortable with both the person and the belief which underlies the use of their hands on our body. Neuro-skeletal realignment therapy sounds like a reasonably safe treatment, but it is always worth exploring a little deeper when we are putting our lives, literally, into someone else's hands. A practitioner recently described the therapy as very holistic, predominantly working through the central nervous system but also affecting the meridians and other etheric systems, and with a close association with acupuncture. Not all therapists practicing neuro-skeletal realignment therapy would necessarily agree with this description, but some clearly do.

To think about: How clean, from a spiritual point of view, are the hands of those offering to massage our bodies to bring health, however well-intentioned?

Therapist or medium?

We briefly looked at reiki earlier in this book. Let's look a bit deeper. The word *reiki* relates to spiritual power. This therapy originated in the 1920s in Japan, apparently given to a man called Usui by revelation, during a time of fasting and prayer. The foundational belief is that there is a universal healing life force which can be accessed through a process called "attunement" carried out by a reiki master. Three degrees of training improve the ability of the practitioner through the attunement process until he or she becomes a reiki master, able then to teach others.

The practitioner's hands are placed on or near the patient, and the universal and intelligent healing energy is said to flow to the place of need in the recipient. The reiki healing can also apparently be carried out at a distance by those with sufficient attunement; this is sometimes called "absent healing." Although there has been no scientific support for the treatment, many people who have used this therapy have reported an improved condition. If there is healing energy coming into the patient then clearly the practitioner is acting as a channel of that spiritual power. For the Christian this is dangerous territory. The practice has some interesting similarities with Biblical healing methods, but reiki acknowledges no authority in Jesus, does not recognize the true gifting of the Holy Spirit, and certainly takes no account of sin. When we put ourselves into the hands of a spirit medium, however well-meaning, we open our lives to the powers of darkness and in particular to demonic spirits of false healing.

Hypnotherapy may seem less likely to be affected by spiritual beliefs, but again we need to think carefully about the spiritual authority under which we might be placing our minds. Hypnotic techniques have been used for mystical and healing purposes for thousands of years. More recently a man called Franz Mesmer, from whom we get the word "mesmerized," pioneered the modern use of hypnotism in seeking to treat human disorders. Hypnotherapy is the use of an altered state of consciousness in the patient, induced through techniques controlled by the therapist, in order to establish new patterns of thought and behavior. The procedure requires a significant surrender of will to the hypnotherapist and this is where the concern lies. If we submit our minds to someone in this way, we are allowing ungodly control over our soul and we can find ourselves wrongly bound both to the treatment and also to the practitioner. God never intended that we should let another person have such control over any part of our mind and our will. The ongoing effects of hypnotherapy in an individual are very uncertain and there have been a significant number of reports of people experiencing personality changes and oppression.

We remember one incident that we experienced a while ago. Sheila had sought help from a hypnotherapist for treatment with an alcohol addiction. She found some release from the difficulty with alcohol, only to find that, some months later, she was struggling with a new eating disorder. It was not until Sheila sought Jesus for freedom from the ungodly control of the hypnotherapist that she was able to find true healing from these recurring addictions, and also from the root issues of emotional damage.

Again it is important to emphasize that it is very unlikely that there was any ill intent by the practitioner, but any altered state of consciousness, particularly if controlled by another person, makes us both emotionally and spiritually very vulnerable. It was clear, as we prayed for Sheila, that she was experiencing deliverance not just from the therapist but also from a demonic spirit which had empowered a *change* in symptoms, but not a *healing* from the root issues. It was actually a spirit of false healing, blocking the true pathway of restoration that God desired for Sheila.

The confusion of science and beliefs

Franz Mesmer, who carried out his experiments into the spiritual forces of healing during the eighteenth century, was particularly interested in the effects of magnetism. Magnetic therapy is still widely used today in a number of different forms. It is believed, by those advocating this treatment, that the human body can experience beneficial effects when placed within an external magnetic field using static magnets or electro-magnets. Indeed the body itself produces small magnetic fields, which some see as means of assessing health. There is very little evidence of any therapeutic effect from quantifying or manipulating these fields, but magnetism is a real and measurable force and there should be no obvious reason to expect harmful spiritual side effects.

However, Franz Mesmer and many other alternative healing practitioners over the centuries have connected magnetic energy fields with unseen healing power that is frequently associated with spiritual concepts such as auras and a universal life force. If certain magnetic fields are proven to have a positive or negative effect on the body, it is important that this is not confused with non-scientific New Age thinking. For example, biomagnetic therapy, a term and practice developed by a doctor of acupuncture several decades ago, uses magnets placed on the body, but this treatment also has strong links with practices such as meridian therapy and homeopathy.

To think about: Is my therapist using a mixture of both safe and unsafe practices, when considered from a spiritual viewpoint?

Summary

Many of the alternative practices used in diagnosing disorder in our bodies are based on forms of divination which are supposed to determine the condition of the energy fields in and around the body. This so-called assessment of energy balance or flow actually relates to an evaluation of our spiritual condition. The Bible makes it clear that our true spiritual condition is actually a consequence of sin and how we have dealt with it before God. None of the alternative methods of diagnosis or treatment is based on that belief. When seeking spiritual restoration, we need to make very sure we are on safe ground.

We need to be alert to the dangers of therapies involving touch and massage, which are intended to impart healing but may actually be opening our lives to spiritual darkness. We need to be aware that some practitioners, without any desire to do harm, may be acting as spirit mediums rather than instruments of health and well-being.

The world of alternative therapies may include pendulums as a useful tool for checking out our healing needs. However, God sees the plumb line of His truth, as given to us in His Word, as being the true way to determine what is out of line in our lives, compared with His righteousness.

Let's move on to look at alternative medicine that we take *into* our bodies, and also the world of meditation, yoga, and martial arts.

Alternative medication

Later in this chapter we are going to take a look at some of the exercise, martial arts, and meditation practices which are founded on spiritual philosophies. However, before exploring these, we want to question some of the medication that goes *into* our bodies rather than the therapies that are carried out *to* our bodies. Whatever goes into our stomach has the opportunity to reach every part of our body, so it is particularly important to be sure that any internal medication is free from harmful side effects.

God has provided an extraordinary array of plants and herbs to bring chemical alleviation to sickness. Many of these have been refined and combined to become the basis of mainstream drugs, bringing huge relief to countless numbers of people over many centuries. Of course, care needs to be taken with the purity and strength of the chemical components of any herbal medication in order that unwanted results don't outweigh the beneficial aspects of the treatment. The problem that we are considering in this book comes when the medication is deemed to have power *beyond* its chemical ability to bring relief to the body.

In the first chapter we looked at Vivienne's story. It was common practice in her family for homeopathic medication to be used to treat every kind of ailment. In fact, for Vivienne, homeopathy seemed to be the supernatural answer to almost every need of healing, until God challenged her one day to see Him as the true source of supernatural restoration.

Many people describe homeopathy as simply a type of herbal medication, but this could not be further from the truth. Because homeopathic medicines are produced through massive dilution of the original plant being used, it is assumed that such dilution must make the treatment a very safe alternative. However, it is the dilution and subsequent shaking process (called "succussion") which is seen, by those preparing the medication, to empower the healing nature of the treatment. Samuel Hahnemann, a Freemason, founded modern homeopathy, believing from his background in Confucianism and Eastern philosophy that disease is the consequence of a spiritual imbalance in the "vital force" flowing through the body of the patient.

Although no pharmacological basis has been shown for homeopathy, Hahnemann formulated a law that says "Like cures like." From this assumption, he looked for plant extracts that seemed to produce the symptoms that he was seeking to cure, and then set about diluting these to such an extent that nothing of the original substance would be able to be found in the final medication. However, he asserted that it then contained the spiritual energy needed for healing. Some homeopathists also use occult methods of diagnosis, such as dowsing, in deciding what particular remedy to use.

Although many practitioners today, including Christian homeopathists, would distance themselves from the spiritual basis of the treatment, there remain profound questions over the source of any healing power experienced and also the spiritual legacy from the deeply occult beliefs of the founder, who was very hostile to any belief in Jesus. Vivienne's experience, when receiving prayer concerning her previous belief in homeopathy, certainly indicated a strong potential for spiritual defilement through this treatment.

To think about: Is it chemical energy or spiritual energy that is being introduced into our bodies through a system of medication such as homeopathy?

Herbal remedies

The careful use of plants and herbs for alleviating sickness is not necessarily wrong. The problem only occurs when we expect the remedy to somehow provide an energy which is linked into the spiritual realms. Bach flower remedies were developed in the 1930s by Edward Bach, a homeopathist. The process is similar to homeopathy, using plant material in extremely weak solutions, although not based on a belief that "like cures like" or that the diluting process gives the medication potency. However, Edward Bach believed that the energy transferred through his remedies from the plant to the patient did produce the healing effect. Actually, apart from water, the only recognizable ingredient of many of the remedies is a small quantity of brandy. The remedies are usually taken orally but can come in the form of creams applied to the body, for skin problems, for example. Edward Bach believed that he had an intuitive understanding of which flowers were needed for each condition. Today some practitioners, including naturopaths, promote dowsing (divining) techniques to decide which remedy to use.

When we previously looked at aromatherapy, we happily affirmed the pleasure of experiencing God-given scents and perfumes, but not the belief that we can benefit from the transfer of some innate energy from a plant into our bodies. Aromatherapy oils are seen by many therapists to bring this kind of energy into our bodies through inhalation or massage techniques. This clearly begins to step into the territory of spiritual restoration and we need to be very sure of what is safe when seeking this kind of healing. We need to be equally careful with traditional herbal medication.

Modern Chinese herbalism is increasingly founded on scientific analysis and procedures for the extraction, purification, and synthesis of plant products. This means that the God-given chemical constituents of plants can be more safely used to restore health, as they have done for many centuries in East Asia. However, when approaching this type of medication, Christians need to be aware of the beliefs of the practitioner. It should be remembered that the historical root practice of Chinese herbalism, when used for medication, was to arrive at a concoction of animal and plant products that was believed to restore the patient's *yin* and *yang* balance.

We should always be willing to question the foundational motive of the practitioner dispensing herbal medication. Is he or she seeking to bring a chemical or a spiritual balance to the body? The problem for Christians is that manipulation of any so-called spiritual imbalance in our lives is nowhere encouraged in the Bible. Our human spirit can be wonderfully restored through receiving Jesus, the Holy Spirit can empower our lives to be more like Him, and unclean spirits can be cast out in His Name. But trying to balance spiritual powers in the body through any technique or medication, however ancient, is a recipe for disorder and not peace.

Natural foods

It makes sense to look for foods that come without lots of additives. People are increasingly objecting to the liberal addition, by many food processors, of preservatives, flavorings, colorings, and sweeteners. Both spiritual and physical food is best when it is without flavor-enhancing additives! When the body, soul, and spirit are fed with pure ingredients, there is every opportunity for healthy living.

The quality of food that goes into our bodies is indeed important, but for some people the search for a pathway of healing can lead them to become obsessed with the issue of food. Almost every day in the newspaper we are warned either of the terrible effects of a particular type of food or the remarkable therapeutic value of another, only to find some time later that the views of the dietary experts have completely changed. The answer seems to be to always pursue moderation in quantity and enjoy a sensible variety of God's amazing provision of good things to eat.

There is also a significant fashion these days in detoxification (detox) regimes to apparently rid the body of all unwanted toxins or impurities, despite the fact that God has designed the body to do this very effectively on its own. All too often, the products and practices associated with detox are based on completely unsubstantiated claims and not infrequently have connections with various alternative remedies. If, for example, we have been poisoning our bodies with too much alcohol, it may well make sense to give the body a time to fully recover, through healthy eating, drinking, and resting. Maybe a little spiritual detox, spending time with the Lord, could be the most effective solution for overindulgence!

To think about: God has provided an amazing variety of food to help us keep our bodies healthy. Has my quest for the right food become an unhealthy obsession?

Exercise

Exercise is good for you! However, as with many of the activities that we are considering in this book, the issue is very often a matter of where we have placed our trust. Spiritual well-being can certainly be enhanced through regular exercise and physical activity. But we should be careful as to what has been given priority in our lives.

We were recently looking at an advertisement outside an exercise gymnasium in the south of England. In bold letters it stated:

My body is a temple
Training is my religion
This is my church
Let me pray

It may be that the phrases were intended to provoke a response and were used simply to attract attention to the facility, but the sentiment expressed is not so far from the truth for many caught up in an obsession for physical fitness.

We remember praying with Philip, a young man who had become addicted to fitness training at his local gym. He was struggling with low self-worth, and bodybuilding seemed to provide an answer to his quest for personal significance. Unfortunately his body had become his idol, and he knew it was wrong. As we prayed for him and asked the Lord to release him from the hold that bodybuilding had over his life, he was surprised at the aggressive and angry feelings that initially rose up inside him in opposition to the pathway of wholeness and freedom that he was now following with the Lord. It was wonderful to see Jesus bring a radical new peace and assurance to this young man. Exercise is an important aspect of our well-being, but we need to take care what pathways of physical training we follow.

Movement therapies often appear with strange names, such as one called "eurhythmy." This technique was invented by Rudolf Steiner, an Austrian philosopher. At the beginning of the twentieth century he founded a new spiritual philosophy out of the Theosophical Society called "anthropophosy." It was a system of beliefs and practice which maintained that by correct training and personal discipline one can attain beneficial experience of the spiritual world. Over the last century, he has been influential particularly in the field of education, where his methods have been seen by some to meet both the intellectual and spiritual needs of pupils. One of Rudolf Steiner's inventions out of this spiritual philosophy was eurhythmy, a movement art used for both performance and therapy.

Once again we need to look at the roots of all exercise and movement therapies to check out the founder and the foundational principles on which the therapies are based. Rudolf Steiner was much more influenced by theosophy than he was by Christianity.

Many exercise regimes these days involve activities related to yoga or Asian martial arts. School classes, evening classes, and youth groups are frequently promoting the merits of these types of training. The spiritual aspects of these practices, coming out of Hindu, Taoist, or Buddhist traditions, do not seem to worry those participating. In fact they seem to be all the more attractive to many people precisely because of the ancient basis of these forms of exercise. We will look at a few of the styles of Asian martial arts later in this chapter; suffice it to say that every style is intended, in some way, to promote both physical and spiritual control of the body. Before we look further at these, let's take a closer look at yoga.

Pamela's story

Pamela had English parents but grew up in a household filled with pictures, furniture, and items of art, all from South-East Asia. Her grandfather had been a diplomat in China, deeply impacted by Chinese culture and philosophy, and he had brought home countless souvenirs. As we talked with Pamela recently, she realized that her parents had shown an almost obsessive liking of oriental culture. Even in Pamela's bedroom there had been pictures of Chinese dragons on furniture and tapestries which hung on the wall. She remembered her father one day showing her a special hidden compartment in one of the statues of Buddha, containing a piece of paper with some sort of prayer mantra written in Chinese characters. Her mother once said, "We don't fully understand the spiritual significance of these things, but we have been told that the objects are believed to bring protection and good luck."

When her sister began to have difficulties with muscle stiffness in her body, it was suggested by a therapist that she start yoga classes. It was seen as a helpful form of exercise to loosen the body and it was not long before Pamela joined in as well. Throughout her teenage years, Pamela regularly attended classes and read books to improve her ability and understanding of the exercise and breathing techniques of a particular branch of yoga linked to Buddhism. In fact, concentrating on the routines of yoga meditation seemed particularly to help Pamela deal with a smoking habit which had developed.

However, she remembered one evening, at the age of twenty, meditating on her own in her apartment when suddenly she felt a very clear touch on her body, although there was definitely nobody else around. The experience had frightened her a little, but she continued to enthusiastically pursue yoga, searching for spiritual as well as physical well-being, until one day someone introduced her to Jesus and she decided to make a life-changing choice to follow Him.

It was not long after her conversion that she began to be increasingly troubled by the effects of yoga in her life. She realized that when praying to the Lord, she felt particularly uncomfortable in adopting the lotus position, a yoga posture she had become very accustomed to using when relaxing. She realized that whenever there were references to China in her life, she became completely overwhelmed with a need to explore oriental culture, through books, food, even Christian Chinese literature and mission stories. Gradually she realized that this attraction to China was not a true calling of God, bringing peace, but a strange and disquieting obsession which seemed to have an unnatural hold on her life.

Pamela decided to ask for prayer. As she and the prayer ministry team sought the Lord for an understanding of how to pray, God reminded Pamela of how, as a little girl, she had particularly loved to play with a little box containing small statues of Buddha. God made it very clear to her that she had in fact spent her childhood in a spiritually unclean house. She loved her parents dearly but began to realize, with sadness, that the Chinese ornaments, idolatrous statues, pictures of Chinese dragons, and other paraphernalia had provided an unsafe spiritual environment which had led her into an obsession with Chinese culture, and with the practice of yoga in particular. She forgave her parents for the spiritual exposure this had caused over her life and she confessed her involvement in the yoga exercises and meditation.

Pamela, now a pastor's wife, recently described to us her remembrance of the prayer time. As she brought the issues before the Lord, she began to feel dizzy and saw clearly a very intimidating vision of a dragon around her. An unexpected and horrible mocking laughter came out of her mouth and she experienced the sense of a snake leaving her body as God brought deliverance from the spiritual powers that had gripped her life. After a little while, she had an overwhelming sense of God's love and an amazing clarity of mind which she had never felt before. She described to us that there followed noticeable progress in her ability to worship, and a significant release into the gifts of the Spirit. Interestingly, she mentioned that she had found a significant change in her taste towards Chinese food, which was hard to describe but very noticeable for her personally. Incidentally, Jesus brought lasting healing for Pamela's smoking problem as well.

To think about: Does my family background make me particularly vulnerable to the spiritual side effects of certain activities like yoga?

Yoga

The practice of yoga is becoming increasingly common as an exercise or therapy, apparently for the improvement of both physical and mental well-being. Pamela had not intended to involve herself in anything more than just some fitness activity. However, the techniques involved had clearly subjected her body to ungodly spiritual control. It may have been that she was more vulnerable than others because of her family's unusual attraction to Asian culture and artwork, but the Bible warns us that when we follow practices which are actually idolatry, there is a spiritual principle which causes us to begin to take on the very characteristics of the idol which we have followed.

> Those who make them [idols] will become like them,
>   Everyone who trusts in them.
>
> (Psalm 115:8 NAS)

Although the practices and positions adopted in yoga are regarded by many simply as a form of helpful exercise, the foundations of the practice of yoga are based on the Hindu belief that, through a series of specific techniques, steps, or stages, we can become spiritually joined to a supreme divine being – the word *yoga* means to be "yoked" or "united" with something. The exercise postures and meditation techniques taught in yoga classes are in fact some of the important stages in this process which together are intended (in the foundational belief) to bring the devotee into oneness with Shiva, a Hindu deity. We can tell ourselves that the yoga positions (usually animal postures) are being adopted without the intention of there being any spiritual submission of our bodies, but we are suggesting in this book that such a viewpoint is a dangerous assumption.

Kundalini

Strongly associated with the practice of yoga is the concept of *kundalini*, a supposed energy center (*chakra*) located at the base of the spine. This place of personal spiritual consciousness is pictured in Hindu writings as a female deity or a coiled snake, apparently needing to be awakened and brought into unity (by rising up through the energy centers in the spine) with the universal spiritual consciousness. This awakening and divine union is believed to be effected through submission to a guru or through practices such as yoga. We suggest that the traditional and New Age beliefs about *kundalini* are in fact a powerful counterfeit of the teaching of Jesus about the need for each one of us to be born again in our human spirit in order to be truly reconciled with Father God (John 3:5–8). To submit to a teaching of false spiritual awakening, through the concept of *kundalini*, is to open a door to the enemy to establish a demonic power that deceptively offers spiritual enlightenment and divine union. It will be a place of harmful bondage and not a pathway to peace.

Pamela is quite certain now that when she sat as a teenager in her room meditating in a yoga position, she was in fact unwittingly opening up her life to unclean spiritual powers. Through this demonic intrusion, she had actually taken on some of the characteristics of false deities associated with Buddhism and yoga. She remembered the powerful impact and disquiet of that touch on her body, and she only felt truly free when Jesus brought His cleansing, through her confession of sin and her forgiveness of those in the family who had pointed her to a false pathway of healing.

Pilates

Pilates is a very widely used method of exercise and physical movement designed to stretch, strengthen, and balance the body. It was founded by Joseph Pilates who was born in 1880; from his study of yoga and Zen meditation, as well as Greek and Roman philosophy, he developed fitness techniques which he initially called Contrology, now known as Pilates. This is one of those practices which again presents Christians with an interesting question. How much spiritual influence does the founder have now on those continuing to follow his techniques? In other words, when we put our bodies into the shapes that Joseph Pilates advocated for our well-being, is it possible that we can today place ourselves under an ungodly spiritual authority which is evident in his belief system?

We looked earlier in this book at the significance of spiritual inheritance when we walk in the footsteps of the founding father of a particular group, practice, or belief. Although he taught many commonsense ways of keeping fit, Joseph Pilates believed Contrology to be a complete coordination of body, mind, and spirit. He also wrote in his book *Return to Life through Contrology*, "So in your very commendable pursuit of all that is implied in the trinity of godlike attributes that only Contrology can offer you ... we wish that your efforts will result in well-merited success chained to everlasting happiness for you and yours."

The intentions of Joseph Pilates may have been very well-meaning, but his philosophies remain contrary to the Bible, which says that *Jesus* is the only way to find abundant life and a true and lasting spiritual health in mind and body.

And that you be renewed in the spirit of your mind, and put on the new self, which in the likeness of God has been created in righteousness and holiness of the truth.

(Ephesians 4:23–24 NAS)

Of course, modern Pilates may seek to distance itself from the spiritual beliefs of the founder, but it is still frequently linked to other alternative therapies and exercises, particularly yoga. A number of the exercise positions and breathing techniques in Pilates come directly from yoga; for example, the cobra position used in yoga is called the "swan" position in Pilates. We are suggesting that it is important for Christians to be cautious, while not being fearful, in deciding what exercise regimes are spiritually safe for them to use.

To think about: In Matthew 11:29, Jesus says, "Take my yoke ... and learn from me ... and you will find rest for your souls" (NIV). Is there a warning here against seeking healing through a false yoke as offered in the practice of yoga?

Martial arts

Listening to the radio recently, I happened to hear a pleasant-sounding young man describe his experience of martial arts. The program was not presented from a Christian perspective, but I was amazed to hear him say the following: "I have been involved with martial arts for a number of years. I consider myself to be a normal, nice sort of guy, but when I step into the contest ring I become a different person. I seem to take on a warring spirit."

Of course, in spiritual terms, this is exactly what is being promoted by many of the techniques employed in the various styles of the martial arts. Essentially, the purpose of many of these techniques is to spiritually empower the body to perform beyond its natural ability. When we invite supernatural power into our body, outside the boundaries of God's commands, we give license to the enemy to have a measure of control. The result can seem appealing to those searching for significance in their lives, but it is actually a place of harmful bondage.

The term "martial arts" can refer to any systemized style of fighting and there are a huge number of styles originating from many different countries. For the purposes of this book, we are considering just a few of the styles which are frequently adopted as techniques for promoting health, in particular Asian martial arts, often with origins in Buddhism or Taoism. People participate in martial arts, usually under the direction of an instructor and often involving an opponent, sometimes for sport, sometimes to promote a healthy body, and sometimes to train for self-defense. The different styles use striking with the feet (such as kickboxing and tae kwon do), striking with the hands (such as karate and tai chi chuan), wrestling and throwing your opponent (such as judo and aikido), and striking with weapons (such as kendo and ninjutsu).

The terms "hard" and "soft" are also applied to styles of martial arts. A hard style (such as kickboxing) seeks to meet force with a stronger force, whereas a soft style (such as judo) will seek to deflect or unbalance the strength of the opponent in order to gain advantage.

One of the surprising things worth noting in the styles given above is the number of times the name of the practice includes the ending "-do." This is a translation of the Chinese or Japanese character meaning "way" or "spiritual path," just as we saw earlier in the philosophy of Taoism (or *Dao*ism). This clearly reminds us that many of these martial arts have developed out of a belief that the training techniques involved are not just physical activities but in fact pathways for supposed enhancement of the whole body, soul, and spirit.

To think about: In John 14:6 Jesus says, "I am the way." If we follow the training of a technique such as judo, even as an exercise or a sport, are we actually being drawn along a spiritual pathway which is opposed to that of Jesus?

Let's look at a few examples of these martial arts styles in order to explore the main issues which we need to consider.

Aikido and tai chi chuan

Aikido provides a good example for us to consider the underlying principles. It is a Japanese martial art developed by a man called Morihei Ueshiba, out of more ancient practices such as ju-jitsu, in the early 1900s. This practice would most often be described as a soft style, seeking to redirect the force of an attacker rather than meet it head on. A reasonable translation of the name would be "the pathway of uniting with the life force." Followers of this pathway are learning how to fight, with or without weapons, in such a way as to attain a sort of harmony with one's opponent so that neither is hurt by the encounter. Although this may seem a laudable principle, we need to understand that Morihei Ueshiba was greatly influenced in the development of aikido by beliefs based on Shintoism, the traditional pantheistic religion of Japan.

Traditional aikido essentially depends on the devotee learning from the instructor how to manipulate and balance the life force (*ki*) flowing through both himself and his opponent. It is intended not only to bring success in combat but also to bring an increasing spiritual well-being to the student.

We are probably most familiar with the practice of tai chi chuan from seeing pictures and films of groups of people in Chinese city parks going through the slow arm and leg movements that form part of the training associated with this martial art. However, the practice can now be found throughout the world. In the British news just recently, there was a report of a dispute between an Anglican vicar and some of his parishioners who were upset that he had banned the tai chi classes in the church hall, because he believed the practice to be incompatible with the teaching of Jesus. Was he right? Along with yoga, tai chi is apparently one of the fastest-growing fitness activities in the United States.

Although the roots of tai chi chuan are as a soft-style martial art from Taoist tradition, the practice has long been proclaimed to bring health benefits to the whole body through the associated movements, breathing exercises, and meditative techniques. The name *tai chi* refers here, not to the *chi* life force, but to a Taoist philosophy of an ultimate combination of the opposing forces of *yin* and *yang*; the word *chuan* relates to the use of the fist, as this practice is founded on a hand-combat technique. As an exercise, the slow repetitive movements give a meditative focus for the mind and a supposed calming effect to the body. However, the classic techniques of tai chi are strongly associated with the spiritual beliefs of traditional Chinese medicine, which saw the balancing of spiritual energy within the body as the basis for health and well-being. This is not the teaching of the Bible.

To think about: Harmony and balance within the human body are good objectives, but can these truly be attained without addressing the sinfulness of the world, which Jesus said He came to take away?

Judo

Recently we had a phone call from a distressed mum: "My seven-year-old son wants to join in the judo class at school. Everyone else is doing it and he'll be so upset if I stop him. The teachers say that it's just good exercise and that I'm making him the odd one out."

Oh, how hard it is for Christian parents to know where to draw the line in giving godly boundaries to our children! We don't want to spoil their fun, but we do want to keep them from harm. The important thing is that parents should be able to make their decisions with sufficient understanding, as well as prayerfully seeking God's direction. We tried to give this mum a little understanding of this particular issue.

We shared with her the basis of judo as viewed by one influential non-Christian practitioner and commentator. In his description he explained that judo had gone through many phases of development, some emphasizing the combative and some the philosophical aspects of the practice. However, this particular commentator ended by affirming his belief that judo was indeed a union of activities of body and soul, containing spiritual and physical factors put together.

The word *judo* means "the way of submission" or "the gentle way." Like aikido, it is a soft style that comes from roots in the martial art of ju-jitsu, an ancient Samurai combat technique without weapons. These techniques almost always followed philosophical as well as practical paths of training. Judo seeks to encourage a submissive style of fighting that draws the opponent off balance.

It is seen by many people today as useful exercise and a way of self-defense, with the result that training classes have become very popular around the world. However, the founder, Jigoro Kano, saw the techniques of judo as an important way of personal self-control and moral growth, which could be followed outside the confines of the combat arena. As with many of the martial arts, the practice of judo combines rituals, progressive ranks or degrees of ability and knowledge, together with an underlying philosophy of self-improvement – all of which do not sit well with the teaching of Jesus. He claims that He is the *only* way that brings true righteousness.

Meditation and relaxation techniques

Meditation has become increasingly popular in Western culture over the last few decades, not least because of The Beatles' contact in the 1960s with Maharishi Mahesh Yogi. He was the guru who developed Transcendental Meditation, a technique for attaining spiritual enlightenment based on Hindu beliefs. Meditation also forms a significant part of many systems of yoga, including hatha yoga, the most common form of yoga practiced in Western culture. In fact many religions (Buddhism in particular) encourage meditation as a means of apparently finding relaxation, peace, enlightenment, and spiritual harmony. The Bible reminds us that it is sometimes only in stillness that the presence of God can be really known.

Be still, and know that I am God ...

(Psalm 46:10 KJV)

Finding a regular place of stillness in our busy lives is a very important part of our pathway to healthy living. However, the method by which we find that stillness can make the difference between true or false peace. We need to be wise. There are countless relaxation therapies using movement, visual, and verbal techniques, many based on Eastern and New Age philosophies. For example, qigong or chi kung, meaning "to work with the universal life force," is similar to tai chi but is not a martial art. It is described as an internal meditation technique using certain postures and breathing techniques to improve the flow of *qi* (*chi*) through the body. Traditionally found in Taoist and Buddhist monasteries, the practice has gained much favor as an aid to health, based on similar principles to acupuncture.

Some procedures for meditation will clearly have an occult foundation, but we need to be alert to less obvious methods that could still be harmful. The question to ask is, "What is the focus of my meditation?" Many techniques encourage us to empty the mind. Be careful! The Bible does not tell us to do this. If we let our minds dwell for any length of time on nothing, we may well be giving opportunity for the enemy to fill the void.

Some systems of meditation use mantras; these are sounds, words, or phrases repeated in order to help connect with the spiritual realm. The roots of this technique are in Hinduism. Both the sounds and the repetition can induce a hypnotic condition where the mind is again out of the control of the person meditating and open to an unguarded spiritual realm.

Sometimes the focus is on visual objects to provide a doorway to meditation. Looking at one thing for a while, like a picture, can indeed be an aid to concentration, but again we need to be careful that this does not become a device that unintentionally hands over the activity of our minds to wrong spiritual powers.

Christian meditation is not about giving away control of our minds. It is about dwelling in the truth of God's Word and letting His Spirit guide our will into choosing what is right, and so bring us to a place of peace.

> *In conclusion, my friends, fill your minds with those things that are good and that deserve praise: things that are true, noble, right, pure, lovely, and honorable. Put into practice what you learned and received from me, both from my words and from my actions. And the God who gives us peace will be with you.*
>
> (Philippians 4:8–9)

Summary

We have taken a closer look at some alternative practices involved with medication, exercise, and meditation. God has encouraged mankind to explore plants to provide relief for sickness, varieties of exercise to strengthen the body, and prayerful meditation to commune with Him. If we look for the restoration of our bodies in careful agreement with the teaching of Jesus, there is much healing that can come through each of these activities. However, there is a deceiver, whom Jesus calls the "ruler of this world" (John 14:30), and he seeks a place of spiritual authority in our lives by encouraging us to follow pathways of restoration which may be governed by the powers of darkness.

It is important that we take care to look at the roots and the founders of all treatments and exercise regimes that we intend to use, in order to check the belief system on which the practice is based. Most practitioners are well-meaning and sincere in their promotion of a particular therapy or style of fitness training. However, they can be deceived, and we are called as Christians to recognize that the gateway of spiritual safety is narrow and it is easy to be led off the right path.

> *Go in through the narrow gate, because the gate to hell is wide and the road that leads to it is easy, and there are many who travel it.*
>
> (Matthew 7:13)

We now need to take a closer look at the nature and the tactics of the enemy.

Believing lies

> *You belong to your father, the devil, and you want to carry out your father's desire. He was a murderer from the beginning, not holding to the truth, for there is no truth in him. When he lies, he speaks his native language, for he is a liar and the father of lies.*
>
> (John 8:44 NIV)

One of the foundational concepts of the Bible that we frequently find ourselves teaching in Ellel Ministries is that truth brings freedom. What a contrast to the basic principle upon which the enemy operates! His motto could be described as "Lies, Lies, and More Lies." In the passage from John's Gospel quoted above, Jesus is very direct in stating that Satan has no truth in him and indeed he is described as "the father of lies."

We will find, therefore, that many things in this world appear to be sound and true, but are actually based on falsehood. When significant numbers of people accept the enemy's lies as their truth, others also believe on the basis that "not all these people can be wrong, surely?" He is then able to exercise power over many as they give him authority in their lives, albeit unwittingly. The apostle Paul recognized this when he urged the Ephesian Christians to be very careful how they lived:

> *So be careful how you live. Don't live like fools, but like those who are wise. Make the most of every opportunity in these evil days.*
>
> (Ephesians 5:15–17 NLT)

Paul saw that they were being lured into beliefs and practices which were deceptions and in fact came from the realm of darkness. Peter also tells his readers that children of light need to be on guard against the devil's schemes (1 Peter 5:8). In other words, be careful what you believe and what you act on. For Christians, the best thing is to base our lives on the teachings of God's Word, and to ask the Holy Spirit to give us discernment in order that we can recognize the lies of the enemy when they present themselves.

When we are considering alternative healing pathways we do need to be very careful that we understand the truth of what's behind them. What seems to be a sound practice of healing may actually be based on a whole set of false presuppositions and beliefs, when seen from God's point of view. Praise God that His truth can indeed set us free when we become embroiled in the falsehoods of the enemy and that He can bring healing to any damage which may have resulted from such involvement.

We were talking to a pastor friend just recently who was telling us about his experience of false healing. Before becoming a Christian, he had gone to an occult spiritual healer for a back problem and had found some relief, but had still been regularly troubled by severe bouts of pain over many years. He received Jesus as his Savior and sometime later received baptism in the Holy Spirit. While this filling of the Holy Spirit was happening, God convicted him of the false healing, and after repentance he found himself completely healed, without any problem since that time. The enemy hates it when his deceptive ways are exposed. Let's look at a couple of these common lies.

A first myth

One of the biggest lies of the enemy, in relation to healing, is that if something seems to make us feel better, it must be all right. This myth is present in much of the morality of Western culture today: "If it's OK for me then it's OK." With such a philosophy, there is no objective standard on which to base our actions. Pragmatism is not always a safe way. We are reminded in the book of Revelation that Satan leads the whole world into error, and promoting such undiscerning attitudes is part of this strategy of the enemy.

> That ancient serpent called the devil, or Satan, who leads the whole world astray.
>
> (Revelation 12:9 NIV)

When concerns are expressed about some alternative therapies in a book like this, there will be controversy, as many people will say that they have been helped by such practices. They may well ask us "What is the problem?" The same approach has sometimes been applied to the taking of an illegal substance to relieve chronic pain. The issue is a complex one even from a worldly viewpoint, as concerns are raised about the use of illegal drugs, the chemical side effects, and so on. However, the deeper spiritual issue is not always considered. When people give some control of their bodies to any type of drug, they would be wise to ask who or what is actually given spiritual authority over them. It is so important to prayerfully consider before God all medical treatment that we follow, whether it is prescribed by a doctor or not. The most important question should be, "Is this treatment consistent with the lordship of Jesus?"

When people get involved in certain alternative therapies, particularly where an unknown healing power is invited, it is surely even more important to ask: "Who or what is then controlling that part of their lives?" This is particularly relevant for those who have chosen to surrender their lives to Jesus, but very often such a question is not even considered. The enemy sits back in his web of lies and surely rejoices at the naivety of many of us when we fail to look out for his fingerprints over the treatment being offered, simply believing the myth that it must be safe if it makes us feel better. Providing a measure of false healing is not difficult for the enemy and this can be the very opportunity that the powers of darkness are able to use to get a little grip on our lives.

Who or what takes charge when we allow a follower of Taoism to manipulate parts of our body supposedly to balance spiritual energy, or when we take into ourselves some medicine prepared in the belief that there is an unseen power at work through that substance? What rights are we giving the enemy by permitting a fitness instructor to direct the movements of our body, when that person may be in agreement with the underlying philosophy of yoga, which seeks to attain a unity with the deity Shiva?

To think about: What things do I do because they seem to work, without really considering who is the spiritual authority behind them?

A second myth

Another lie that permeates the world of alternative healing is the concept that if something is "natural" it must be safer and probably more beneficial than medicine which has been chemically synthesized. The term "natural" seems to give us a sense of comfort, but we must be careful not to be misled. Many plants contain powerful toxins, and many substances that are found in the natural world may be safe in certain quantities but must be used with extreme caution. Opiates are used for pain relief but carry strongly addictive properties. If you have too much of certain vitamins it can actually be harmful. Even drinking too much water can sometimes cause damaging over-hydration of the body.

Many naturopaths, for example, believe in the inherent healing power of nature and that by avoiding mainstream medication and surgery there will be a more successful restoration from sickness. However, for Christians, their foundational belief is that all healing power comes from God, while at the same time acknowledging that He has provided an amazing variety of medical skills and chemically helpful substances. Of course many of these substances come originally from plants and sometimes animals.

The natural world of God's creation is given to us for our enjoyment and well-being. However, there is no hint from the Bible that God has imbued either plants or animals with therapeutic qualities of unseen healing energy beyond the chemical and nutritional content which He has provided for us to discover. In fact, the Bible tells us to be wise with God's wisdom when we are considering what we rely on, not just accepting the views of others who may naively tell us that an alternative medication must be OK because it is "natural."

> *This wisdom is not that which comes down from above, but is earthly, natural, demonic. For where jealousy and selfish ambition exist, there is disorder and every evil thing. But the wisdom from above is first pure, then peaceable, gentle, reasonable, full of mercy and good fruits, unwavering, without hypocrisy.*
>
> (James 3:15–17 NAS)

Beware of fantastic claims

The enemy is adept at unreality and fantasy. In our desperation to find an answer to our healing needs, we can find ourselves surprisingly willing to believe the unbelievable. The cure-all claims made by some alternative remedies should ring alarm bells for us. Here are some examples of the claims made by some practitioners that we have come across:

> *Pilates is a complete coordination of body, mind, and spirit.*
>
> *If you guide your body correctly it will vitalize and heal itself almost immediately.*
>
> *Aromatherapy is a modern scientific way to bring emotional tranquility and beauty into people's lives.*
>
> *With a touch on the body's energy centers, relieve respiratory problems, weaknesses of the immune and circulatory systems, stress, migraines, and other common complaints.*
>
> *Six keys [from the Kabbalah] to physical and spiritual healing can lead us toward perfect health.*

These claims may be very appealing, but we need to be wary of following pathways of unreality. The more we have faith in something or someone, the more spiritual authority and power we give them over our lives. Many New Age therapists will say that their remedy only really works when the client is in a place of full submission to the particular practice. Ill health can make people desperate for a cure and it is tempting to discard our spiritual discernment in the hope of finding something that will meet our needs.

We remember Peggy, who told us about a chronic back problem she had endured for many years. "There came a point," she said, "when I was ready to try anything, I was so desperate for some relief." She went on to explain that she had been encouraged to try both homeopathy and acupuncture, even though she had felt uncomfortable about both treatments. She had experienced a little relief but no lasting cure. She now felt the need to confess to the Lord that she had looked in wrong places for her healing and was shocked by the strong deliverance that she experienced as she asked the Lord to cleanse her from any unhelpful effects of the therapies. She described the feelings of a powerful grip on her spine that was suddenly released. She told us that she knew that now God's true healing could begin to flow into her body.

The enemy's desire to control

Authority is the *right* to exercise control. Before the Fall of man, God delegated spiritual authority to mankind to govern His creation.

> *[God] blessed them, and said, "Have many children, so that your descendants will live all over the earth and bring it under their control. I am putting you in charge of the fish, the birds, and all the wild animals."*
> (Genesis 1:28)

Power is the *ability* to do something. God empowered mankind to carry out the work of governing His creation. With authority and power, there is then the opportunity to control the things over which we are given charge.

The main desire of Satan, the enemy in this world, is to exercise his own control. If he can gain spiritual authority over someone, he can use his own power in and through them for his purposes. When mankind fell from the place of perfection through the sin of Adam and Eve, spiritual authority was surrendered by mankind to Satan, as ungodly choices were made to follow his deceptive instructions. Satan already had power, as a supernatural being, but with the Fall he could then use that power through men and women as they effectively gave him the authority to control their lives and also the world around them. The enemy continues to look for ways to perpetuate that control.

Whenever we choose to give away some of the authority which has come from God, we give a right of control to those to whom we give that authority. An ambassador in a foreign land has the authority of his homeland to act on its behalf. However, if there is no recognition of that authority by the rulers of the country in which he lives, he remains powerless. On the other hand, if his authority is backed up by the military might of his homeland, it is likely that he will be taken far more seriously in his role as ambassador!

Authority *with* power is able to change things for better or for worse. When we give Satan rights over us by our submission to things which are not godly, he can gain control over us in these areas. Any alternative ways of healing, which are in some way governed by ungodly spiritual powers, can give Satan rights of control over those who become involved in them, however unpleasant that may sound!

Demons are the powers of darkness that Satan has under his command. He uses them to hold onto control where he has been given rights in people's lives. Much of the ministry of Jesus was involved in dealing with these powers and so re-establishing the rightful authority of God in the lives of men and women who recognized the truth of His words.

> *But if I cast out demons by the Spirit of God, then the kingdom of God has come upon you.*
>
> (Matthew 12:28 NAS)

To think about: Have I let the enemy get some control in my life during any part of my search for healing?

Whose power has stood the test of time?

We have mentioned that it is common for promoters of alternative therapies to point to the antiquity of their practices as a validation for the process. If it is so old, they argue, it must work! However, we should remember that God is a lot older than any earthly process. Before any of the Eastern therapies were thought of, before Taoism or Confucianism began, before the Indian Vedas were written, God had already declared in His Word that He is the true source of healing:

> *... I am the LORD, who heals you.*
>
> (Exodus 15:26 NIV)

Throughout history the enemy has offered countless remedies to our need for healing, but not one of them will ever be founded on the importance of getting our lives right with God, by recognizing man's sin and the wonderful forgiveness that comes through Jesus Christ. True Christian healing is the safest holistic therapy.

False healing with a "Christian" label

> *For false Messiahs and false prophets will appear; they will perform great miracles and wonders in order to deceive even God's chosen people, if possible.*
>
> (Matthew 24:24)

At Ellel Ministries we passionately believe in the healing and deliverance ministry of Jesus. We have the privilege of seeing many precious Christian brothers and sisters find life-changing wholeness and freedom as they respond to the prompting of the Holy Spirit, in bringing their lives increasingly under the lordship of Jesus. We will look more at His pathway of healing for our lives in the next chapter.

However, the verse above contains a dramatic warning that, as we approach the last days, there will be false miracles, with Christians believing that they have received restoration from Jesus but actually finding themselves deceived and even put into bondage to the evil one. It seems that his deceptive tactics will become more and more subtle.

Whilst seeking the true work of Jesus in our lives, how do we guard against healing practices which may have a Christian label but are actually defiled by the enemy's intrusion? Thankfully, the Bible not only warns us of the problem of deception, but also gives many guidelines, teaching us how to be sure that Jesus is in rightful control of the pathway of restoration for our lives.

Avoiding the enemy's deception

Here are some suggestions for safety guidelines that we can apply as we interact with other people in churches and ministries, especially when healing and deliverance are being offered:

1. If we have taken time to know the true voice of Jesus, He says that false healers will seem like strangers to us.

    A stranger they simply will not follow, but will flee from him, because they do not know the voice of strangers.

    (John 10:5 NAS)

2. Is the character of Jesus, the *fruit* of the Holy Spirit, seen to be growing in those ministering, however impressive we consider the *power* displayed?

    So then, you will know them by their fruits.

    (Matthew 7:20 NAS)

3. Without bringing condemnation, is sinful behavior clearly addressed in the teaching and ministry?

    If we say that we have no sin, we deceive ourselves, and there is no truth in us. But if we confess our sins to God, he will keep his promise and do what is right: he will forgive us our sins and purify us from all our wrongdoing.

    (1 John 1:8–9)

4. Is the divine order and balance between Father God, Jesus Christ, and the Holy Spirit clearly acknowledged in the teaching and ministry?

    Who, then, is the liar? It is those who say that Jesus is not the Messiah. Such people are the Enemy of Christ – they reject both the Father and the Son.

    (1 John 2:22)

5. If we earnestly desire the Lord to gift us with the ability to discern spirits, the Holy Spirit will empower us to know what is false, when this is needed.

    But it is one and the same Spirit who does all this; as he wishes, he gives a different gift to each person.

    (1 Corinthians 12:11)

False pathways of healing, through those claiming to have the anointing of the Holy Spirit, will be part of the enemy's lies, especially in these last days. We do not need to be fearful of this but simply watch out for the true teaching, the true character, and therefore the true authority of Jesus. Healing power is safe when it is under right authority. The enemy may counterfeit impressive power but he *cannot* grow the fruit of the Holy Spirit in people's lives.

But the Spirit produces love, joy, peace, patience, kindness, goodness, faithfulness, humility, and self-control. There is no law against such things as these.

(Galatians 5:22–23)

To think about: Am I sufficiently alert to the deception that Jesus has warned us of in these last days?

Getting wrongly tied to other people

Surely you know that when you surrender yourselves as slaves to obey someone, you are in fact the slaves of the master you obey – either of sin, which results in death, or of obedience, which results in being put right with God.

(Romans 6:16)

The enemy can also exercise control over us through ungodly relationships. These can be established not just through issues like sexual immorality, but also through unwise relationships with those who purport to offer us help and healing.

Throughout our lives we have many times followed the instructions, the advice, or the leading of other people. Very often this will have been absolutely right, resulting in necessary provision and protection for our lives. However, the verse above reminds us that when someone has authority over us in some way, it has an unseen or spiritual consequence. There can be a lasting tie, even as strong as the bond which would exist between a slave and his master. This may be good or bad, life-giving or destructive, depending on the godliness of the relationship. These unseen ties are sometimes called "soul ties." There is another book in the Truth & Freedom series which deals particularly with this concept.

Where others have controlled us or we have surrendered ourselves to others in a way that has given them wrong authority and power over our lives, the unseen ties can remain a source of spiritual bondage, stealing the abundant life and true healing which Jesus came to give us. When we come under the direction of a therapist, instructor, or provider of an alternative remedy, we are putting ourselves under their authority. We should ask the questions, "Under what authority am I placing myself?" "Are their methods consistent with the lordship of Jesus?"

God desires that ultimately *He* should be our Master, directing and nurturing our lives. He will never coerce us into being His slaves, but He does give us the freewill choice to respond to His unconditional love, and to serve Him for eternity. Where other relationships, past or present, have tied us to wrong masters, freedom is readily available through repentance of our own sin, forgiveness of those who have had wrong authority over us, and asking the Lord to release us from the spiritual captivity.

To think about: Who might I be tied to in a wrong way because of my choice of healing paths in the past?

Soul ties in alternative healing practices

Let's explore this idea a little further. Suppose we go to an alternative practitioner offering, for example, Thai massage. The practice is based on a belief in the therapeutic manipulation of energy pathways (*sen*) in the body. Let's suppose that the practitioner is also engaged in Buddhist worship and the practice of yoga. When he or she is involved in their personal worship and yoga, they are affirming the spiritual authority of Hindu and Buddhist deities over their life, and seeking to align themselves with the spiritual powers in those religions. This means that they are becoming agencies of gods which are certainly not the God and Father of the Lord Jesus. In fact, according to the Bible these gods are simply demons, seeking to control human lives.

> *No! What I am saying is that what is sacrificed on pagan altars is offered to demons, not to God. And I do not want you to be partners with demons.*
>
> (1 Corinthians 10:20)

By subjecting our bodies to this masseur we have placed our life, in part, under their spiritual control. We have allowed the possibility of our being tied to both them and indeed to the false gods that they worship, in an unseen but powerful way. An ungodly soul tie not only binds us to another person, but provides a pathway of spiritual darkness that can be used by the demonic powers operating in the one to whom we have become tied. These unclean spirits may be able to counterfeit a measure of healing but will usually bring further bondage and block the true path of God's restoration for our lives. In other words, if we have accepted the false healing as the answer to our needs, we have denied God the opportunity to bring His true wholeness and freedom. It's another one of Satan's strategies to lead us astray.

The experience of Ellel Ministries is that as we share these truths with people who have been deceived by false healing, God is only too willing to bring His freedom. If they repent, receive forgiveness through the Name of Jesus Christ, and the soul ties with the practitioner are cut, then amazing spiritual and emotional freedom is experienced, often with true physical healing following.

We had just such an experience, some while ago, when a Christian man came for prayer for a shoulder problem. During our conversation he revealed that he had previously received Thai massage for a short time, although he had not been comfortable with it and eventually asked the practitioner to stop. From then on, he had had all kinds of difficulty with his shoulder. We prayed about the therapy and he repented of his action, forgave the practitioner, and was loosed from the tie. The next morning he reported that his shoulder was undoubtedly better even before we had the opportunity to pray specifically for physical healing.

The enemy wants us to be dependent on anything but God!

We mentioned earlier in this book an issue that frequently seems to be associated with alternative therapies, namely dependency. It's another way that Satan can build his control over us by making us wrongly dependent on those to whom we go for help. This of course can be a problem even in the church community. If people start relying on their pastor, or someone else in the church who is particularly kind and understanding, especially if their prayers appear to be effective, then the dependence on God is impaired. Satan likes this human-centered behavior because it distracts us from the centrality of God.

When the dependency also involves false healing, the enemy not only benefits from the lack of a focus on God but also from the increasing demonic control that this can permit. It seems that many of the alternative therapies, exercises, and treatments can become almost addictive for some people, who even fear what would happen if they stopped. When there is a friendly therapist who is interested in me and seems to care about me, it is easy to see how this can begin to take an emotional hold on me, especially if I have experienced rejection in my life. When this emotional dependence is combined with treatment that has an occult basis, it is not long before a spiritual hold can also begin to get a grip. It then becomes an opportunity for the enemy to establish a strong soul tie which can pull me away from my true Savior.

Of course there can also be dependency issues with mainstream drugs. The chemical side effects of some medications include the problem of addiction. Usually the doctor prescribing the medicine will carefully take this into account when deciding the right treatment. Sometimes the alleviation of difficult symptoms requires strong drugs to be taken for a while. It is always helpful to ask Jesus to be Lord of all that we need to take into our bodies, seeking His guard on anything that might take a wrong hold on us, both chemically and spiritually.

Jesus wants us to remain dependent on Him, both in the medication we take and in our relationships with those helping us along our pathway of healing. As we grow in our trust of Him, we will discover that His gentle hold will never do us harm.

To think about: In my quest for healing, have I become wrongly dependent on someone or something without realizing it?

Some thoughts on treatments for the mind

In looking at the realities of healthcare, we need to be aware of the possible danger that exists with some of the mainstream treatments that are prescribed for mental disorders. There is still a great deal which is unknown about the way the mind works, and some of the medication and procedures that have been developed to help those with sickness of the mind can have spiritual consequences as well as the physical and emotional results intended. Some psychiatric techniques have possibilities of ungodly control over the mind which we, as Christians, should be concerned about.

Carl Jung, an influential Swiss psychiatrist who was practicing during the early part of the last century, was deeply involved in the occult and believed that all kinds of spiritual exploration and experience were an important part of the pathway to healing of the mind. Psychiatric care has gone through considerable development since his time and this is certainly not to say that all psychiatry is wrong. However, we should be wary of treatments which might challenge or change the spiritual order within the human body which God has put together. Careless treatment of the mind can give opportunity for enemy activity.

Electric shock treatment, or electroconvulsive therapy, for example, appears to cause some form of dissociation within the individual which effectively disconnects them from the dysfunction being treated. However, with this level of trauma to the body, brokenness within the human spirit is very likely to result and leave a lasting issue of inner damage. Sometimes such treatments are used with well-meaning intentions as a last resort in a desperate situation, but serious thought and prayer needs to be entered into by the individual and the family of anyone considering such treatment.

In the same way, some strong drugs prescribed for mental health issues may well produce spiritual brokenness and personality changes, even though they may appear to control other aspects of sickness. We remember praying for Irene who had been given a very powerful drug to deal with serious anxiety issues in her teenage life. Although she had not taken the medication for many years, it became clear during the prayer time that the chemical trauma to her body caused by the drug had deeply affected the spiritual integrity of her body. Thankfully, God brought a powerful restoration of wholeness and freedom as Irene put this part of her life into the Lord's hands. It is always best to seek the Lord for wisdom, and indeed protection, when we find ourselves needing medical help to manage the distressing symptoms of mental sickness.

Once again, the addictive nature of some anti-depressants is also well recognized. It may be argued that the addiction is better than the depression, but if we believe that God can and does heal depression, which may have a spiritual root in issues such as unhealed childhood injustice or trauma, such medication should be approached with caution. Of course clinical depression may well be the result of a chemical deficiency in the body, and medication may be helpful to redress the balance. However, prayerful preparation should be made in such circumstances, as God may want to show the truth of the emotional or spiritual damage which lies at the root of the chemical disorder.

> *Praise the* LORD, *O my soul,*
> *and forget not all His benefits –*
> *who forgives all your sins*
> *and heals all your diseases.*
>
> (Psalm 103:2–3 NIV)

Keeping under God's protection

In order to know the blessings of the Almighty God in our lives, we must remain under His spiritual covering. As part of the extended faith family in Jesus Christ, we benefit from the protection and provision of our Heavenly Father. He is able to fulfill His covenant promise of healing power in us, through His authority as our God. From the beginning of creation mankind came under this protection, but due to the Fall the spiritual covering was usurped by the enemy. From that time, whenever God's people sinned, they stepped outside of God's covering and brought the spiritual hostility of the enemy upon themselves and upon the families for whom they carried responsibility.

> *The few of you who survive in the land of your enemies will waste away because of your own sin and the sin of your ancestors.*
>
> (Leviticus 26:39)

Of course, now there is the opportunity of God's forgiveness and restoration through all that Jesus has accomplished for us. However, by pursuing ungodly pathways of healing we can be putting ourselves outside the spiritual covering of the Lord and thus become vulnerable to the power of the enemy working in us. Where the founders of alternative therapies have promoted false spiritual healing, we can be exposed to an ungodly spiritual inheritance where we have joined in the spiritual family of those father figures. God intended that His children should walk in the blessings of the family of God through Jesus Christ, not in the cursing of spiritual families founded on deception.

The solution is to reaffirm our desire for God's authority in our lives, to pray for Him to reveal to us where we may have stepped off His pathway, to ask His forgiveness, and thus to re-establish the authority and covering of God over us. There may well be a change of behavior required as a consequence, in order to ensure that we remain under God's protection for the future. A lady came to us recently for prayer. During her early life she was involved in many occult practices and false religions. Following her conversion to Christ, through lack of good teaching and her continuing unhealed problems, she became involved with a number of alternative therapies. It seemed as if she was still walking under the effects of an unprotected and hostile spiritual inheritance. This had resulted in much damage and bondage in her life. It was wonderful to see that through repentance she was able to be released from this area of spiritual vulnerability and be delivered and restored into a right place with the Lord.

Sickness and sin

We have been considering some of Satan's strategies in the area of alternative therapies, but we need to emphasize the fundamental truth which is avoided by them all. It is the essential difference between the holistic practices of alternative medicine and the spiritual restoration that comes through faith in Jesus Christ. The Biblical view of sickness is that it is the consequence of the imperfection in creation resulting from the Fall. Before Genesis 3, mankind was as originally created: good, and formed in the image of God, who is perfect. After the Fall, when sin had entered into the life of man, sickness and death appear as the normal experience of human beings.

In order to truly deal with sickness in this world, sin must also be dealt with. We know as Christians that only Jesus Christ provides the solution for sin, and it is only through His Name that salvation and restoration can be achieved. No other alternative therapy either recognizes sin as an issue in the process of healing, or indeed has any means of dealing with sin. The world of alternative medicine has seen the dysfunction of body, mind (soul), and spirit, but only Jesus can provide the true solution.

The healing and deliverance ministry of Jesus truly complements conventional mainstream medicine because He is the only One who can deal with the root cause of sickness and so bring true freedom and wholeness to our lives. Our spiritual resurrection life, which begins with our salvation now and is completed in heaven, also contains the potential for healing through the God and Father of our Lord Jesus Christ.

For as in Adam all die, even so in Christ all shall be made alive.
(1 Corinthians 15:22 NKJV)

To think about: Have I been trying to get solutions for my problems through therapies that are not able to deal with the root issue of the sin of mankind?

Summary

Satan is a liar and we must be on our guard against his subtle deceptions when we are considering anything which promotes healing methods which could be outside of God's promises. Because something seems to work it doesn't necessarily make it right. We must look at the spiritual authority and power behind the process which is promoting healing. The enemy can bring a form of healing but it is always at the price of more of his control and it never results in true wholeness or freedom.

When we submit ourselves to a holistic therapy which is conducted under a spiritual authority not consistent with the lordship of Jesus, we can become tied to the practitioner and thus to those powers of darkness that are operating through this person. Dependency and spiritual bondage can be the result. Thankfully, Jesus came to bring freedom where we have been caught by the enemy's schemes. Treatments which are directed towards reordering the mind are to be carefully considered as they can often have a spiritual as well as physical effect within us. They can compound the problem rather than solve it.

The fundamental issue with sickness is the sin in mankind and this is only dealt with through the cross. Unless a pathway to healing acknowledges this issue, true restoration of body, soul, and spirit cannot be complete or lastingly effective. Awareness of the enemy's strategies must not lead to fear, but it is important to recognize his seductive ways ...

> *... lest Satan should take advantage of us; for we are not ignorant of his devices.*
>
> (2 Corinthians 2:11 NKJV)

CHAPTER 8
Jesus – the
Safe Alternative

Looking for the safe pathway

> *Thus says the LORD,*
>   *"Stand by the ways and see and ask for the ancient paths,*
>   *Where the good way is, and walk in it;*
>   *And you will find rest for your souls ..."*
>
> (Jeremiah 6:16 NAS)

So far in this book we have raised serious questions about alternative ways of healing, and we have expressed our concerns regarding their origins and spiritual safety. We are very sure that sickness is real and also that people can get healing from a number of different sources. Mainstream medicine brings relief for a large number of physical conditions, but many people recognize that it doesn't address the inner needs of the person. Throughout history, mankind has tried to find his own way in this quest for holistic healing. The Bible warns us about going it alone.

> *There is a way which seems right to a man,*
>   *But its end is the way of death.*
>
> (Proverbs 14:12 NAS)

121

Alternative therapies and medicines are being increasingly used worldwide and even endorsed by some government authorities. However, we have sought to show that a significant proportion of these alternatives ways of healing have dubious spiritual roots and are sometimes downright dangerous for the Christian to engage in. So is there a safe alternative way which truly complements and addresses the limitations of mainstream medical practice in Western culture?

Our answer is a categorical *yes*! Jesus Christ, Son of the Living God, is *the* safe alternative to the lack of wholeness and freedom in human experience. He is the true Healer of the body, soul, and spirit.

A light in the darkness

The conversion experience is often parodied in the media with the phrase "I've seen the light." Nowhere in Scripture is anyone recorded as having said that, although the apostle Paul refers to a light which shone into his darkness on the road to Damascus (Acts 26:13). In fact this light preceded the physical darkness (Paul's temporary blindness) which resulted from that encounter, but spiritual darkness had been with Paul for all his life up to that point.

On an earlier occasion Jesus had met a man born blind from birth who was miraculously healed by the Lord. His testimony was that he had been blind and now he could see (John 9:25). Many people have found that the only way to describe their newfound faith relationship with Jesus was to say they had indeed "seen the light." For the Christian, the state of being outside of Christ is as if we were in darkness, and the new condition of being in Christ is like being in the light. It is interesting that so many non-Christian religious and spiritual journeys are described as a quest for enlightenment.

The hard part for many who are not yet in God's Kingdom is that they are in darkness but don't know it. Jesus offers light, but they can't yet see it. As a consequence, the world that lives under Satan's rule doesn't recognize the spiritual darkness and the danger that engulfs it. The therapies and treatments that are not consistent with the lordship of Jesus are, by His definition, in the realm of darkness. Those who are of the Kingdom of light, yet offer practices surrounded in darkness, are in reality both being deceived and promoting deception. Paul points out the incompatibility:

> *What fellowship can light have with darkness?*
>
> (2 Corinthians 6:14 NIV)

To think about: Am I compromising my own faith by being involved with things of darkness which I should be avoiding?

Jesus gets to the roots

We said in the last chapter that the fundamental issue behind all sickness of body, soul, and spirit is that of the sin of mankind. We have noted that any holistic therapy which attempts to deal with the symptoms, without looking at the true causes, is bound to be incomplete and possibly carrying unhelpful side effects. The root of all sickness is sin and only Jesus Christ can get at that root effectively and permanently. So how does He do that?

Christian belief states that Jesus was fully man and is fully God. As such, He alone could act on our behalf in taking the place of mankind by paying the penalty set by God as the consequence of sin. God had said to Adam that to break His rule would be to suffer death. Paul applies this to all sin and makes it very clear that ...

> *... the wages of sin is death ...*
>
> (Romans 6:23 NIV)

Since that initial disobedience set the pattern for all of mankind, whereby anyone who breaks God's Law is guilty of sin and deserves to die, it is only by the offer of a similar all-encompassing life that all can be set free from the consequences of the sin. These consequences are vulnerability to the enemy's hostility and disorder in the human being, which include sickness. Sickness of our human spirit, resulting from damaging choices by ourselves and others, leads to sickness of soul, affecting the mind, will, and emotions; and this in turn is frequently manifested in sickness of the body. The only solution is to go back to the root and put right the wrong.

Jesus cannot change the fact that Adam and Eve sinned but He has dealt with the consequences in His representative role, as Son of Man and Son of God, by dying in our place. As a result, the hold which Satan had over mankind through sin is broken, which opens the way to a holistic restoration of our whole being. Through Jesus' representative death on the cross, those who come to Him in repentance and faith are forgiven by the Father, who no longer demands the penalty to be paid by us. We can stand in the authority of His Son, Jesus Christ, against the activities of Satan and live in freedom. This includes the potential for freedom from all sickness. Again Paul sums this up by referring to the Fall of man and the resurrection of Christ.

> For as in Adam all die, so in Christ all will be made alive.
>
> (1 Corinthians 15:22 NIV)

From restored roots comes abundant fruit

Jesus told us that He has come to bring us life in all its fullness. His disciples interpreted His teaching as meaning that this new life starts now, here on this earth, and their ministry illustrated

this truth as they prayed for the sick in the Name of Jesus and
saw abundant life given through healing.

At last, in the place of darkness caused by the inevitable sin
of mankind, a light shone out, whose name is Jesus. His own
description of Himself was "the way, the truth, and the life"
(John 14:6) and it is by knowing the truth of Jesus and His way
that a life of freedom can result.

You will know the truth, and the truth will set you free.

(John 8:32 NIV)

As Jesus restored the relationship with the Creator God by
dealing with the sin that separated us from Him, so He restored
the connection through which the healing power of the Father
could flow into the lives of His created children. Once more
the healing character of God, Yahweh Rophi, God the Healer
(Exodus 15:26) can be experienced by us as we come to Him
in the Name of Jesus. This is the true healing that responds to
mankind's heart cry for inner peace, heard throughout history.

Any form of holistic healing without the authority of Jesus
can never secure a permanent solution; indeed a cynic might
say that it is in the therapist's interest if there is not complete
healing, as that generates more income! When Jesus died on
the cross He did so once for all, thereby dealing permanently
and eternally with the problem of sin. The healing of the
relationship with God is everlasting, and the power of God is
eternal, so we can expect that when God does His work in us
that too will be everlasting and eternal. His grace is such that
often He will challenge us and heal us in progressive stages, so
that it can even seem as if the sickness returns. In reality once
God has healed us, it is permanent, unless we turn our back on
His healing. We may become sick again through other causes,
including the inevitable deterioration of the physical body
but, once forgiven and cleansed, that sin is dealt with forever.
Hallelujah!

We should always remember that life is not just this physical existence on earth. The final healing comes for believers when they are released from the earthly body to receive a new spiritual body which endures in the presence of God for eternity. Whatever alternative therapy is offered for restoration in this life, it will not ensure the life to come, whereas Jesus truly brings abundant and eternal life.

To think about: Do I have an eternal perspective on my life, as well as my desire for physical well-being today?

People of the Way

Taoist philosophers, along with countless others down through the ages, have been searching for a pathway of living that would bring peace and harmony to human existence. In Christ Jesus we have found it, or rather we have found Him who *is* the Way, the only spiritual route to Father God, the Creator of the universe. What an extraordinary privilege to have been given the answer to this ancient quest!

When Paul was still operating in spiritual darkness he knew that those who were following Jesus were a threat to the religious legalism on which he had built his life. He believed that there was something very dangerous about this new spiritual pathway and about those who were called "people of the Way," – the followers of Jesus.

> *In the meantime Saul kept up his violent threats of murder against the followers of the Lord. He went to the High Priest and asked for letters of introduction to the synagogues in Damascus, so that if he should find there any followers of the Way of the Lord, he would be able to arrest them, both men and women, and bring them back to Jerusalem.*
>
> (Acts 9:1–2)

Jesus is the Way, the perfect alternative to the world's philosophies, for all our spiritual needs and restoration. It's no wonder that the enemy wants to tempt us to venture down blind alleyways and dead ends. Satan's ways are many, but not one leads to abundant life. In His mercy, God will look for us even on any wrong spiritual pathway which we have taken, but He will only ever point us to the one true path that is Jesus.

> *Jesus answered him, "I am the way, the truth, and the life; no one goes to the Father except by me."*
>
> (John 14:6)

How Jesus brings healing

We have previously mentioned that the model for healing on which we have based the work of Ellel Ministries is that of Jesus as seen in Luke 9:11. In this verse we are shown that there are three parts to Jesus' ministry: welcoming, teaching, and healing. In our centers we seek to offer a warm welcome to guests and to teach Kingdom truths, and the healing that is then offered flows from this, through prayer.

> *... the crowds ... followed him. He welcomed them and spoke to them about the kingdom of God, and healed those who needed healing.*
>
> (Luke 9:11 NIV)

There are some clear principles that Jesus used when He was engaged in His healing ministry. As we seek healing for one another, these principles will be as relevant for us today as when Jesus walked the earth. Let's consider a few of them. The first one, and the most important, is that of *forgiveness*. When we look at the story of the paralyzed man who was let down through the roof into Jesus' presence, we see that Jesus did not initially speak about the paralysis of the body, but rather the sickness of the man's spirit. It was as a result of the forgiveness of his sin that the man was subsequently able to walk (Luke 5:17–26).

There are numerous occasions when people who come to our centers for ministry discover an area of unforgiven sin, either done by them or done to them. When they are helped to enter into God's forgiveness, it is amazing the changes that take place as they are set free from the bondages of guilt, shame, or bitterness that previously existed. Forgiving others and receiving God's forgiveness for our own sin removes all the rights (the spiritual authority) that the enemy has used to bring harm to us through the iniquity that has affected our lives.

Linda, who had been born in China, came to one of our centers complaining of chronic knee problems. During a teaching seminar, God reminded her of the day, before she had been a Christian, when she had visited the village Buddhist temple to seek healing for her father. She remembered saying, as she had knelt before the temple priest, that she was willing to endure the sickness herself if her father could be healed. She realized as she now reflected on the incident that she had cursed her own body and had given particular rights of sickness over that part of her body (her knees) which had demonstrated submission to the demonic powers ruling over that temple. As she confessed her sin, forgave the deception of the temple priest, and received God's forgiveness and cleansing for herself, she was wonderfully delivered and healed of the problem in her knees. There surely is an enemy who prowls about looking for those he can devour (1 Peter 5:8).

This is clearly another principle that we see in the ministry of Jesus – that of *deliverance*: the removal of the enemy's authority and power. In Luke 13 we see a woman who met Jesus, having been crippled by an unclean spirit for eighteen years. He called her over to Him and released her from her infirmity. In the ensuing discussion with the synagogue ruler about what had happened, Jesus made it clear that her freedom was the result of her being freed from the bondage of Satan, even though Jesus regarded her as being a "daughter of Abraham" – in other words, a covenant child of God. There are often times in our ministry in Ellel centers when it is evident that there is some demonic occupation which is affecting a person, and the pathway of God's healing requires that the powers of darkness are challenged and expelled.

A third important principle from the Gospel record is that Jesus acted with supreme *authority*. Again in the story of the healing of the paralyzed man who was lowered through the roof by his friends, Jesus declared to the Pharisees and teachers of the law that He had "authority ... to forgive sins" (Luke 5:24). The healing of the man was a consequence of the change of spiritual authority in his life. By facing reality and embracing the principle of forgiveness, the lordship of Jesus could be established. Today, the Christian healing ministry is effective only when we are operating under God's spiritual covering. This requires our being in a right relationship with Jesus. It is only under the supreme authority of His Name that we have any power to heal the sick or to confront the powers of darkness.

To think about: As a disciple of Jesus, am I prepared to walk in His authority and power to bring true healing to a needy world?

The Spirit of God

Jesus now operates through a new body: the Body of Christ on earth. That Body is empowered to carry out the healing ministry of Jesus through the dynamic activity of the Holy Spirit, as He imparts the gifts referred to in the New Testament. The Spirit is in no way separate from God; indeed He is part of the Triune God – a third person of the Trinity. Therefore anything that we say of Jesus must be related to the Spirit and vice versa. When

Jesus died to pay the price of our sin, so the Spirit was present as the power which raised Jesus from the dead. He *is* the life in our mortal bodies.

> *And if the Spirit of him who raised Jesus from the dead is living in you, he who raised Christ from the dead will also give life to your mortal bodies through his Spirit, who lives in you.*
>
> (Romans 8:11 NIV)

When the Father supernaturally works healing in our bodies through the exercise of spiritual gifts, the Holy Spirit does not then move off to work somewhere else and leave us "discharged" from His interest. The Spirit searches all things, we are told in 1 Corinthians 2:10, even the deep things of God. He certainly therefore knows and understands our real needs, the true source of our sicknesses, and how to bring us into wholeness. There are many occasions when the Spirit works first in the inner being before He releases physical healing into the body.

We know of a lady who was seriously disabled through multiple sclerosis. As part of her journey with God, she received much ministry in inner healing from the Spirit of God, through the agency of prayer from others, over a period of several years. One day she was prayed for regarding her physical illness and received a miraculous healing, such that there is now no evidence in her body of her former illness. That was over two decades ago.

She's deeply thankful to God for her physical healing, but often says that the inner healing was, in a sense, the more profound as it seemed to prepare the way for the later miracle and the lasting freedom that she now enjoys. The Holy Spirit was active throughout the process, while the Name of Jesus was the authority by which the healing of Father God was effected. All true Christian healing depends on this amazing divine protocol within the Godhead.

To think about: Healing through the Spirit of God involves the dynamic and personal intervention of God in our lives, unlike the impersonal life force that is invoked in many alternative therapies. The enemy simply wants to impose control, whilst Jesus desires most to be known.

Only one Lord

We have been affirming that Jesus is our safe alternative when looking to receive deeper healing beyond the limits of mainstream medicine. As we seek His authority and power, it's good to remind ourselves that Jesus really *is* Lord. Theologically this is true, but it also needs to be a reality in our daily lives. It is no good our singing that "We trust in Him" if we don't behave in a way that confirms this. We can't sensibly dabble in those alternative remedies which are subtly proclaiming other powers and even other gods, while at the same time declaring the lordship of Jesus in our lives.

There is a challenging saying: *Either Jesus is Lord of all or He is not Lord at all.* A prayer that we often use in prayer ministry at Ellel centers is one we call "the Lordship Prayer" and in it we encourage guests to speak out that Jesus is Lord of every aspect of their lives. By doing this they are beginning to undermine any areas of authority in which Satan has managed to get the upper hand and are moving forward into getting a right order restored. The prayer will be found in the next chapter of this book. It is a simple matter to speak out words of allegiance to Jesus, but it is another thing to really mean them. So often, we find that we have taken back the control of the circumstances of our lives and then we wonder why things start to go wrong. True healing can only be found when Jesus is restored as Lord.

Because Jesus is the Son of the Living Creator God, there is no higher power or authority under which we could live. Because of God's totally loving nature, He will never do us harm and is completely trustworthy. By putting the sicknesses of our body, soul, or spirit in Jesus' hands we can be sure that we are safe and will be dealt with lovingly and permanently, even though there may be a period of time during which the process of wholeness and freedom takes place. When Jesus is in control of the journey of our life, it is like walking under a firm but easy yoke, guiding us to the place of peace for which we have yearned. His way carries no harmful side effects, but instead a growing experience of His love.

> *Come to me, all of you who are tired from carrying heavy loads, and I will give you rest. Take my yoke and put it on you, and learn from me, because I am gentle and humble in spirit; and you will find rest. For the yoke I will give you is easy, and the load I will put on you is light.*
>
> (Matthew 11:28–30)

To think about: Have I strayed outside the safety of the spiritual authority of Jesus? Am I walking under yokes that are wrongly controlling my life?

Summary

Human existence outside of a true relationship with God is in spiritual darkness. Jesus alone takes us along the pathway of God's light. The root problem behind all sickness is the fallen state of man through the sin that began in Adam and Eve. Only Jesus can get to the root of the problem and make a difference such that we are no longer subject to the penalty of sin or bound to the spiritual authority of Satan through that sin.

In the ministry of Jesus we see three particularly important principles, namely forgiveness, deliverance from the enemy, and the supreme authority of Jesus. The Holy Spirit is the supernatural agency of the power of God in all healing, and without His activity true healing cannot take place.

In order to receive the fullness of God's restoration, we must recognize that Jesus needs to be Lord of all that we are and all that we do. We can't put part of our healing needs under alternative spiritual authorities and, at the same time, declare the lordship of Christ over our journey into wholeness and freedom. Only in Jesus can we find the safe alternative healer to complement mainstream medical treatment, which itself has also been given by God to help relieve suffering in this world. Let's look now at how we can make sure that we are on the right path: His pathway of healing.

Finding Freedom and Wholeness

True restoration – the character of God

God has given amazing understanding to man in the whole area of medical diagnosis and treatment. Much suffering has been relieved through the study and use of drugs and surgical procedures. We have been affirming that at the root of all sickness is the spiritual disorder which exists in God's creation through the sin of mankind and the breaking of covenant with his Maker. God has made available a unique way for that covenant relationship with Him to be restored. It is only through Jesus, the Savior of mankind, that the spiritual disorder in this world, and also in our individual lives, can be made right. When Jesus said, "I am the way, the truth, and the life" (John 14:6), He was warning us that other pathways of spiritual restoration are not safe and do not bring the abundant life that He so desires for each one of us.

Have we, maybe without realizing before, been on a wrong path? Have we followed a way of healing that was outside the safe boundaries of God's plan for our lives? Straying off the narrow path can mean that we have stepped into enemy territory, experiencing spiritual side effects which have not brought true freedom but in fact a place of bondage.

Go in through the narrow gate; for wide is the gate and broad is the way
that leads to destruction, and many are the ones entering in through it.

(Matthew 7:13 LITV)

God's love for each one of us is not affected by the mistakes that
we have made in our lives, but something of His blessing is lost
when we stray outside His spiritual covering. The great news
is that, through Jesus Christ, the covering can be completely
restored. Recognizing that we may have moved into the enemy
territory of false healing need not be a place of fear, but simply
an opportunity to let the True Healer take us by the hand and
return us to the right path.

We mentioned earlier that there is a growing fashion these
days for following a detox diet regime, apparently to rid the
body of harmful chemical toxins. More importantly, what about
spiritual detox? There are probably many Christians who would
question the need for cleansing our bodies from the effects of
spiritual defilement. However, the Bible sees such cleansing as
an important part of the process of getting right with God in
those areas where we have wandered off His straight path.

But if we confess our sins to God, he will keep his promise and do what is
right: he will forgive us our sins and purify us from all our wrongdoing.

(1 John 1:9)

To think about: When God shows us things that have been
wrong in our past, it is because He wants to put it right for
our future.

Facing the truth

It is not the intention of this book to persuade Christians that
they have been wrong in their choice of ways of healing. It is
the Spirit of God who convicts us of where our past mistakes

are affecting our lives today. Many times when teaching about this subject, we have found that people have had a personal awareness of particular remedies about which they no longer feel comfortable. Sometimes they have expressed a sense that their lives have remained somehow tied to a particular therapy or practitioner in a way that has left them without peace, even if the therapy seemed to bring a measure of relief at the time.

We had exactly that experience just recently with a man who had sought healing, some years ago, through the practice of reiki. During a time of prayer, he began to feel strongly that God was now showing him that this therapy had had a negative effect on his life. As he renounced the choices which he had made and asked God to release him from the wrong hold which the treatment was having on his body, he was amazed to find himself experiencing a strong deliverance. A powerful new sense of peace and purity then filled his whole being. We are never condemned by the gentle voice of God, only convicted to see the truth as He sees it. Mistakes are not a problem for God to deal with, if we are open to Him. It is only persistent rebellion that blocks God's redeeming work in our lives.

Alternative therapists are not bad people

We told the story of Vivienne in the first chapter. Her father believed that homeopathy was good for his family, but it became clear to Vivienne that he was mistaken and had been deceived by an artful enemy who provided only false healing together with unseen side effects of spiritual bondage. Jesus told us that the enemy is the "father of all lies" (John 8:44) and we should not be surprised at his tactics to mislead both ourselves and also those who are seeking to help others. Christian therapists are not immune from this deception. A Christian label does not secure a godly spiritual covering. Seeking God's righteousness is a daily challenge for each one of us as we look for His guidance in the journey of life, particularly at those times when we have deep needs and any answer can seem better than none.

When our lives are subjected to the instruction or control of others, we need to be especially careful to seek the Lord for wisdom. If their practices are sinful in God's view, we can find ourselves damaged by the experience and trapped by the enemy, even if it was never our intention. Jesus came to bring wholeness and freedom to a damaged world. He delights in our receiving restoration under His direction and protection.

A checklist

Below is a list of simple questions which might prompt thoughts on whether our lives have been adversely affected by the spiritual side effects of alternative ways of healing which were outside God's protection. Remember, it is much more important to listen to what God is saying rather than get caught up in detailed self-analysis, but the following reminders may be helpful.

In the therapies, remedies, or exercises that you have experienced:

1. Was there any reference made to life force or energy levels, flows, blockage, or transfers in the body?
2. Was there any mention of altered or alternative states of consciousness?
3. Did the therapy include anything to do with the body's aura or energy fields?
4. Did the expressions *chi* or *ki* appear in the name or literature of the therapy?
5. Were there references to meridians or *yin* and *yang*?
6. Did the therapy mention the Vedas, yoga, or Zen in its use or foundations?

7. Was there a process involving the therapist's hands moving over parts of the body, even without actually touching it?

8. Were certain locations of the body given particular importance, while not seeming to be connected to the problem area?

9. Did the therapy include the use of essential oils?

10. Were questions asked about your spiritual condition or star signs?

11. Was diagnosis apparently dependent on the study of one part of the body in particular, such as the tongue or the eyes?

12. Did the diagnosis use methods or instruments that seemed strange for determining your physical condition?

13. Was there encouragement to concentrate or to empty the mind in a particular way to help dispel the sickness?

14. Did the exercise or postures require particular meditative procedures or mental submission to another person?

15. Did the treatment process leave you feeling a bit unsettled in your spirit, or even include things which you know were contrary to Scripture?

16. Was fascination part of your reason for doing this therapy?

17. Was the explanation of the therapy confusing?

18. From literature around the premises, was the therapist involved in alternative therapies apart from the one you were receiving?

The challenge of righteousness

We were speaking to someone who felt that such concern about the spiritual side effects of alternative therapies and practices was too extreme. It is certainly very important that looking at a subject like this does not bring us into a place of fear or obsessive self-analysis. That would play right into the enemy's hands. However, under the New Covenant with mankind, Jesus challenged His followers to consider God's view of what is right and wrong in a completely new way, moving well beyond what they had previously considered as acceptable rules.

> *You have heard that people were told in the past, "Do not commit murder; anyone who does will be brought to trial." But now I tell you: if you are angry with your brother you will be brought to trial ...*
>
> (Matthew 5:21–22)

This would have been very shocking for the disciples and must have seemed an utterly impossible standard. Surely this was "over the top." But Jesus is well aware that our own attempts at righteousness can never achieve this level of purity. It is only possible as we let Him live more and more in us and through us, by His Spirit. Jesus never condemns us for not being like Him; He simply wants to bring conviction to the next part of our lives which needs to be brought into submission to His ways.

As we take time to look seriously at our lives, all He asks is that we listen to His voice concerning the truth of those things which might still be harmful to us or, as He said to His disciples in the passage above, might be bringing us "to trial." Jesus is very concerned to help us to surrender to Him every area of our lives, especially where the enemy seeks to hold us in any place of accusation and punishment. Our involvement in harmful alternative therapy is not necessarily top of Jesus' list of the things that He wants to tackle in our lives right now. However, we should not be surprised if, at some time, He does bring conviction in this area, in order that another hold of the enemy can be dealt with forever.

It may be that, while reading this book, God has indeed drawn your attention to alternative medication or practices which might have affected your life. We would like to take you through some simple steps to bring these issues before God and seek His cleansing from any harm that has been the consequence of your involvement. There are suggestions for what you can say at each step, with gaps to fill in specific details or names as appropriate. However, we suggest that you let the Holy Spirit direct your thoughts and prayers. It might be helpful to have a couple of Christian friends alongside, to walk with you through these steps.

Step 1 – Affirming the lordship of Jesus

In the last chapter, we stressed the importance of the spiritual authority of Jesus in every part of our being if we are seeking any new step of freedom and wholeness for our lives. His lordship is a process of progressive surrender to all that He says is right about who we are and what we do. It is the only foundation for Christian healing.

A suggestion for what to say (the "Lordship Prayer"):

Lord Jesus, I acknowledge my need of You and accept You as my Savior, my Deliverer, and my Lord. I invite You now to be the Lord over the whole of my life.

Lord of my human spirit and all my spiritual awareness and worship.

Lord of my mind, my attitudes, my thinking, my beliefs, and my imagination.

Lord of my emotions and the expression of my feelings.

Lord of my will and all my decisions.

Lord of my body, my physical health, my exercise, my diet, my rest, and my appearance.

Lord of my sexuality and its expression.

Lord of my family and all my relationships.

Lord of my times of work and times of relaxation.

Lord of my material goods and my perceived needs.

Lord of my finances.

Lord of my plans, my ambitions, and my future.

Lord of my journey of healing.
Lord of the time and process of my physical death.
Thank you that Your blood was shed that I might be free from
the consequences of sin and that my name is written in the book
of life.
Amen

Step 2 – Acknowledging truth

There is always a doorway of truth that we need to pass through
in order to find God's freedom and healing. The enemy hates it
when we discover, and respond to, what God has revealed about
our lives.

> *So Jesus said to those who believed in him, "If you obey my teaching, you*
> *are really my disciples; you will know the truth, and the truth will set*
> *you free."*
>
> (John 8:31–32)

If God is now showing you His viewpoint on a particular healing
issue in your life which you hadn't realized before, then it would
be very good to bring this issue out into the light and begin to
remove the shroud of darkness in which the enemy would want
to conceal any hold on your life. God has determined a pathway
of restoration for all His children and we need to discover those
places where the enemy has enticed us off course and stolen
the true healing that God has for us.

A suggestion for what to say:

> *Father God, You have made it clear in Your word that You desire*
> *blessing and healing in the lives of all Your children. This pathway*
> *of healing is often narrow and there is an enemy who seeks to make*
> *the path crooked and so cause me to stumble.*
>
> *Thank you for the significant help that I have experienced*
> *through godly medical practitioners and treatments. I choose now*
> *to view all the therapies and medication which I have experienced*

in my life as You view them. I acknowledge that the fullness of true restoration in body, soul, and spirit only comes through the fact that Jesus has dealt with the sin of mankind at the cross.

I accept that I have sometimes strayed off Your pathway for my life and, in part, given control of my healing journey to the enemy. I ask that You restore me.

Amen

Step 3 – Confession and receiving forgiveness

It is time to be specific. What particular medication, treatment, or therapy do you sense was not part of God's plan for your healing journey? Who was the practitioner, therapist, or instructor that was given control over part of your life? Agreeing with God is always the starting place for His redeeming work in our lives. Our mistakes are not news to Him. He simply waits for our willingness to agree with Him that He is always right and we have often been wrong!

A suggestion for what to say:

Father God, I confess that I have sought healing, exercise, or therapy in ways that are not consistent with Your spiritual authority and the true pathway that Jesus would want me to follow. In particular I confess .... [name the particular issue being confessed]. I renounce this practice as not being Your way of restoration for my life and I receive Your forgiveness and cleansing from all that has defiled my life in this area. Thank you, Lord, for Your love and protection, in Jesus' Name.

Amen

Step 4 – Forgiveness of others

Having acknowledged your own responsibility for what happened, you need to consider who else was involved. You may not necessarily feel bitter towards those who have led you or encouraged you onto a false pathway of healing, but it is important to acknowledge their sin, even if they were acting in ignorance. When you forgive someone for the harmful effect of their actions on your life, you enter into God's system of justice whereby mercy triumphs over judgment, through the death of Jesus on the cross. Satan, who loves to accuse you and hold you in a place of punishment, then loses his rights, and you can be restored onto the pathway of freedom.

Think for a moment who needs to be forgiven for their control, carelessness, or maybe even for taking advantage of you in your time of need.

The false healing may have been through those practicing alternative occult procedures or may even have been through those claiming to bring Christian healing, but it has now become clear to you that the fruit of the true character of Jesus was not in evidence. Sometimes we also need to forgive those, like parents or pastors, who did not provide the spiritual protection that we needed at the time.

> *And when you stand and pray, forgive anything you may have against anyone, so that your Father in heaven will forgive the wrongs you have done.*
>
> (Mark 11:25)

A suggestion for what to say:

> *Father, thank you for forgiving me for the wrongs which I have done. I now choose to forgive .... [name those involved] for their part in my involvement in .... [name the therapy involved]. I release them into the freedom of my forgiveness.*
> *Amen*

Step 5 – Dealing with soul ties
When we seek therapeutic treatment for our bodies, we often put our life, or at least a part of it, into someone else's hands. This may even be literally, if the procedure involves laying

on hands, manipulation, or massage, for example. This is not necessarily bad, but it is important to recognize the spiritual significance of placing ourselves under the authority of a person who may not have the same beliefs or spiritual awareness as ourselves. A therapist, spiritual healer, or instructor may have had very good intentions of helping us, but if they were acting as a channel of ungodly spiritual power, we may find ourselves tied to them in a damaging way that we never intended.

In hypnotherapy, for example, the client gives control of part of their mind to the therapist. In treatment through reiki, the practitioner is acting as a medium for "healing energy" to be transferred through his or her body into the patient. Certain massage techniques which place the patient under the power of the masseur may be intended to bring a sense of well-being but are very likely, spiritually, to tie the participants in an unhelpful bondage. In martial arts and yoga classes the instructor often takes a position of significant authority in the progress of the participants on the spiritual journey that is part of the intended purpose of the practice.

As well as those with whom we may have had a direct relationship, it is sometimes necessary to look at the origins of the therapy. The so-called guru or founding father of certain belief systems which lie behind some healing practices can carry a powerful control over the adherents to that system, even if the founder is no longer physically alive. Such leaders of false healing practices are in effect acting as false prophets. It is important that we separate ourselves from their influence over our lives.

Once we have confessed our part and forgiven those who have held such control over our lives, we can seek freedom from the Lord for any way in which we have become tied to those who have practiced any form of false therapy or spiritual guidance over us. Matthew 18:18 tells us an important truth:

Truly I say to you, Whatever you bind on the earth will be, having been

bound in Heaven. And whatever you loose on the earth will be, having
been loosed in Heaven.

(Matthew 18:18 LITV)

A suggestion for what to say:

*Father God, as a result of my giving control over part of my life
to .... [if possible, name the therapist/practitioner/instruc-
tor/founder], I realize that I can be spiritually tied to them in a
way that is not helpful. I have confessed my sin in wrongly seeking healing through this therapy and I have forgiven the therapist/
practitioner/instructor/founder for the negative effect that this has
had on my life.*

*As I loose myself from the relationship in the earthly realm, I
proclaim that You, Father, have loosed me, in the heavenly realms,
from all ties that are in any way affecting my body, soul, and spirit.
I ask, Lord, that there would be a complete separation between
that person's life and mine, so restoring my individual freedom
and wholeness.*

Amen

Step 6 – Deliverance from powers of darkness

When the enemy is given spiritual authority, through our
wrong beliefs and behaviors, and through the decisions which
we've made in our lives, he has the opportunity to empower
that authority with unclean spirits. Occult therapies, medication
based on unsafe spiritual principles, exercise regimes founded
on techniques which seek spiritual control of the body, as well
as the soul ties with therapists and instructors, can all give
spiritual authority to the enemy.

The confession and forgiveness in which we have
participated, in the steps above, have the effect of removing the
enemy's authority in those parts of our lives where we have
chosen to bring the light of the lordship of Jesus. It is now time
to dis-empower the enemy's hold by expelling unclean spirits

which may have had a grip on the areas of our lives where we sought false healing or restoration.

> *... in order to keep Satan from getting the upper hand over us; for we know what his plans are.*
>
> (2 Corinthians 2:11)

A suggestion for what to say:

> *I declare that I choose true healing under the authority of Jesus Christ and I renounce all false healing that comes through therapies based on the unseen powers of darkness. Your rights, enemy, over my body, soul, and spirit are removed, and I take authority, in Christ, over every unclean spirit given access through these practices which have been confessed.*
>
> *Spirits of false healing, false life force, mind control, mockery of Christian healing, infirmity and .... [name the likely spiritual powers, such as yin and yang, chi, or Hindu deities, associated with the therapy or exercise regime which has been renounced], I command you to leave my body now.*

Step 7 – Finding true restoration and peace

It has always been a covenant promise of God that He would be the true Healer of His people:

> *He said, "If you will obey me completely by doing what I consider right and by keeping my commands, I will not punish you with any of the diseases that I brought on the Egyptians. I am the LORD, the one who heals you."*
>
> (Exodus 15:26)

False healing restricts the purposes of God in our lives. When the enemy has a place of authority over any part of the healing pathway of our lives, the light of God's restoration cannot fully penetrate. As the hold of the powers of darkness is recognized and removed, there is a new opportunity to find the fullness of healing which Jesus has secured for us at the cross. *He* is the safe path for what the world calls "holistic" healing.

> *Happy are those who know they are spiritually poor;*
>   *the Kingdom of heaven belongs to them!*
>
> (Matthew 5:3)

A suggestion for what to say:

> *Father, thank you for rescuing me from darkness and bringing my life increasingly into the light. You understand my needs for healing and I trust You to lead me on the very best pathway for restoration and peace. I receive today the healing that You have prepared for me, in spirit, soul, and body, particularly in those areas where past false healing has blocked my journey, through Jesus Christ my Savior. Amen*

Finally … open your heart to all that God wants to say and do today. He's supernatural but safe when we submit to His commands and His ways. The journey of wholeness and freedom will continue throughout this earthly life, and finds its completion in our eternal heavenly home. Let's consider how best to walk the journey of this life in as safe a way as possible, alert to the devouring nature of the enemy of souls.

CHAPTER 10
Walking in Safety

There is only one true light

Many years ago a young man we know was taking part in an overnight walk through a large forest as part of an event organized between youth groups in the UK. The walk was being monitored by army personnel to ensure all went well, and each group of walkers was issued with maps, flashlights, and a set of directions in order that all could safely travel from the starting point to their destination.

All was going according to plan, until one group leader, full of the wisdom of youth, decided that as the moon was so bright he didn't need the flashlight; this would enable his group to travel unseen and get ahead of their nearest competitors. Unfortunately, by not referring regularly to the map, he mistook weed on a pond for what appeared to be grass, and disappeared up to his waist in slimy water. His own choice of light and his own wisdom let him down!

This can be the way that many Christians treat alternative therapies. Instead of bringing the light of Scripture and the wisdom of God to bear on that which may seem safe, there is often a complacency which causes them to venture along paths which could well lead into a "miry pit." We have sought to show in the preceding chapters why there should be real concerns for Christians about many of the alternative ways of healing available, in order to prevent the damage that could result.

The better way for a Christian is to walk according to the light of the Word of God, relying on the guidance and illumination of the Holy Spirit for understanding and discernment, rather than human wisdom. The psalmist reminds us of the value of reliance on God's Word:

Your word is a lamp to my feet
and a light for my path.

(Psalm 119:105 NIV)

Let's look at some practical ways to help us to keep out of danger.

Getting cleaned up!

So long as we are walking the path of righteousness, the enemy cannot get a hold in our lives. It is surprising how small the finger-holds are that are needed for an experienced mountaineer to be able to scale an apparently sheer rock face. In the same way, it is shocking how the enemy can use even the smallest opportunity to get a grip on part of our lives. By walking according to God's truth we can eliminate these opportunities.

Godly living is not simply a matter of "dos" and "don'ts." The Old Testament regulations were intended to keep the people of God holy, but we know how unholy the nation of Israel became despite the Law. Jesus came to set us free to do right, not according to Law but according to the Spirit. By deepening our relationship with the Lord, and understanding what is God's heart for His people, we can begin to take on a new lifestyle as the Spirit changes us into the likeness of Christ.

We ... are being transformed into his likeness with ever-increasing glory, which comes from the Lord, who is the Spirit.

(2 Corinthians 3:18 NIV)

The Christian life is like that of a sea bird that gets caught in an oil spill. It may have the happy experience of being rescued by someone out of the blackness and destructiveness of the oil, but it can take a long time and much perseverance to get the oil out of the bird. It can be a long pathway to full recovery and the ability to really fly as God intended. In the same way, we begin our journey as a Christian still carrying much of the spiritual darkness of the past. This can cloud our spiritual vision and dull our awareness of Satan's tactics. It is a very defiling world and we have often gone where God had not intended us to walk. As we embrace the cleansing that God has prepared for our lives, we become increasingly alert to the deceptive ways of the enemy. Our transformation into the likeness of Christ may take time, but what a worthwhile journey!

The New Testament is full of exhortations to holy living. The amazing thing is that it was written to believers who were *not* being holy in how they lived. A Bible commentator recently wrote that we are told there are about fifty-two different unholy lifestyles which Christians are called to avoid – a different one for each week of the year! Becoming Christ-like in our actions and attitudes is a necessary part of avoiding the traps of the enemy and receiving more of our healing.

Just as he who called you is holy, so be holy in all you do; for it is written "Be holy, because I am holy."

(1 Peter 1:15 NIV)

To think about: Are there things in my life that I have done which have given the enemy even a small foothold, and so make me more vulnerable to his deception? This could be a good opportunity to get a bit more cleaned up!

Keeping under cover – God's cover

As we continue in our Christian lives, we come to understand that we are not walking alone. God has formed His people into His Body, in which we have an interrelationship which is intended to edify or build up all who are sanctified in Christ: the born-again believers. Instead of leaving us vulnerable to "go it alone," He has placed in the Body gifted and anointed individuals whose task is "the equipping of the saints" (Ephesians 4:12 NKJV). When the relationships and gifting are rightfully acknowledged in the Body, God's protection (His spiritual covering) is established for all of God's people.

> *It was he who gave some to be apostles, some to be prophets, some to be evangelists, and some to be pastors and teachers, to prepare God's people for works of service ...*
>
> (Ephesians 4:11–12 NIV)

As part of this gifting, God has organized the leadership of the Church to have the particular functions of both pastoral care and also giving direction to the Body. Different denominations practice this in different ways, so for some it is a hierarchical structure and for others a more congregational style, but whatever form leadership takes, it has a significant role in the protection, restoration, and healing of the members of the Body.

God's plan is that no one in His Body should be left vulnerable to the enemy, ever since what happened when the Fall took place and Adam and Eve stepped outside of God's covering. Whilst every adult believer must carry personal responsibility, the leaders of churches and families are given a special task of maintaining God's spiritual covering over those for whom they are responsible, in order to help protect the group from the enemy's attacks. We have seen that the enemy will take every opportunity to devour those who step outside of

God's boundaries of holiness. Whilst Jesus covers His Church from heaven, much of the day-to-day maintenance of that protection is provided through the gifting God has invested in church and family leadership. Sheep are certainly responsible for their foolish wanderings, but much of their safety in keeping on a true path is dependent on the wisdom and leading of the shepherd.

One problem in the Church today is that much of leadership resource is spent running the organization of the Church rather than providing God's direction to the Body. Furthermore there is ignorance amongst some leaders of the vital nature of their covering responsibility. When leaders spend endless time in organizing programs or debating finances, to the exclusion of true pastoral care, their church can be wide open to deception. In people's desperate quest for healing, unsafe alternative treatments can abound among the flock. They can even be condoned by those whose task it is to protect the sheep from deception, because the shepherd does not understand or accept the dangers of giving such ground to the enemy.

This situation is like the father of a family holding up a leaky umbrella over the family; everyone is exposed wherever there are holes, when Dad is careless in his role of providing a sound covering. He needs to get the umbrella repaired by dealing with his sin. We suggest that the best ways for this covering to be provided by church leaders are through sound teaching and the provision of the best alternative therapy: a team administering the healing and deliverance ministry of Jesus. Church leaders need to become involved in the healing ministry and either support what the prayer ministry team is doing, or actively participate as their time and gifting permit. Having the authority of the church leadership behind the prayer ministry is essential for an effective healing program in the local church.

To think about: Apart from my own responsibility, who is providing God's covering for my life to help keep me on the right path?

The place of prayer

How often do you pray before going to the doctor? Do you submit your medication to the cleansing power of God before taking it? Do you ask Jesus before you purchase some new treatment from the pharmacy? What do you think Jesus would want to say if He stood by you in your exercise class or therapy sessions?

You may think that these questions are a bit excessive, but prayer for healing is not only asking for health after we have become sick! Surely we are called to pray in all circumstances, and that must include praying over the conventional medicines we may take, for their effectiveness in our bodies and for protection against hidden dangers. It is a good idea to pray for protection also when we go to visit our doctor or any other medical practitioner, bearing in mind that he or she may be an active follower of another faith. We are mostly unaware of many of the background spiritual dynamics active in the manufacture of medicines, and even if we are seeking to use just the "safe" ones, it is good to ask God to protect us from the Evil One and his works through these preparations. Many of us are happy to say grace before a meal but perhaps this should be extended to everything that we take into our bodies.

To think about: How often do I pray for the medical personnel that usually treat me, for their well-being and for their salvation?

Perhaps the best way is to be proactive in prayer. Pray before embarking on any course of medication or therapy, even if it seems spiritually safe. Ask Jesus to reveal any side effects which you should be concerned about and which may not be obvious – the "hidden things."

> *He reveals deep and hidden things;*
> *he knows what lies in darkness,*
> *and light dwells with him.*

(Daniel 2:22 NIV)

Prayer deals with fears too. We must be careful not to become fearful of every medical process or treatment that we encounter, thinking it might be satanic! If we pray for God's protection and peace, we can go forward in confidence, providing of course that we are not involving ourselves in things which we know to be wrong or dubious. We don't want people, having read this book, to be afraid of going to their doctor or local hospital; we are to live in this world, but we don't need to be part of its spiritual deception if we walk with Jesus.

Being wise and informed is right preparation, but giving a place to fear may just be another way that the enemy can control our lives. God has provided many wonderful resources for the health and healing of the human body. Our concern in this book is that those things which could adversely affect our soul and spirit are made clear, so that Christians can avoid them. Scripture reminds us to remain alert when Peter says:

> *Be self-controlled and alert. Your enemy the devil prowls around like a roaring lion looking for someone to devour.*
>
> (1 Peter 5:8 NIV)

Recognizing realities

A man attended a Christian event and received prayer for healing. His problem was that he had defective vision and wore glasses, as do many people these days, but he believed that as a Christian he shouldn't continue to have this impaired vision. Having been prayed for, he declared that he had received his healing, took off his glasses, and promptly walked into an obstruction he hadn't seen. In his case God hadn't healed him and he was living in unreality!

The fact is that since the Fall, people are not in perfect health physically, and some of that illness continues even to the end of life. However much we believe in God the Healer, and declare our faith in His healing power, there will be some occasions when people remain sick. In the life-to-come after death, when all is made new, sickness will not be an issue. Living as a Christian now may sometimes mean that we have to take natural precautions and live within the reality of our limitations. There are times when we are asked to pray for people who come to Ellel Ministries but we find that they're in denial about the realities of their life. For example, some are looking for God's restoration while inwardly blaming Him for the difficulties that they are experiencing. This can actually prevent healing, as the true condition of their lives needs to be faced before any meaningful prayer can be engaged in.

Sometimes we must face up to the fact that the damage to our human spirit, although originated through the devil's work at the Fall of man, actually comes from the sinful actions of human beings, and is not a direct enemy attack. Those who abuse others may well be acting out of the damage they received through their own dysfunctional childhood or other personal experiences in life, but it is their sinful action that gives ground to the enemy. To seek deliverance from the powers of darkness, without first recognizing the rights given through sin, is unlikely to help. It is like trying to ward off or appease evil spirits by the use of alternative practices, such as feng shui, when this will simply lead to deeper bondage because the real issue of sin has not been addressed.

If the enemy does mount a real attack on our health, then we need to deal with these times through the effective strategy of Christian prayer and deliverance. To try and fix things through the alternative ways of medication or therapy described in this book actually just strengthens the work of the enemy within our lives. Taking an example from the current military conflict in Afghanistan, it would be a bit like an American soldier going to the Taliban to ask for help to win the war.

When Jesus walked this earth He was extremely practical and very real about the situations He encountered, even if His reality was often at odds with that of those He met. The little girl who died and was raised to life (in Mark 5) was perceived to still be dead when Jesus met her. However, the reality of Jesus was that of His Kingdom and He spoke life in the face of death. This was not walking in fantasy but in His knowledge of the truth. On the other hand, the demoniac in Gadara was known by everyone to be severely demonized, and Jesus dealt with him accordingly, by clear confrontation with the enemy (Mark 5:1–20). Our realities need to be, at the same time, both practical and Kingdom-oriented. Jesus has promised that the Holy Spirit will show us what is true, if we let Him guide us.

> *When, however, the Spirit comes, who reveals the truth about God, He will lead you into all the truth. He will not speak on his own authority, but he will speak of what he hears and will tell you of things to come.*
>
> (John 16:13)

To think about: Am I living in reality about my own health and my need for healing?

In whom do I put my trust?

A final issue to mention again is that we can easily become dependent on those who are treating us, even in the ministry of Christian healing. One of the biggest lies for an addicted person is their belief that they can easily do without the substance or the activity. Sadly, some people with sickness can become dependent on either the fact of their illness or on the person who is treating them. This has always been a possibility within the traditional doctor–patient relationship, but because of the intimate care and concern shown frequently by many alternative practitioners, there is a particular danger of dependency for patients who especially want to be accepted and valued.

This danger is growing as the conventional medical practitioners become busier, with bigger patient numbers to cope with and thus less time to spend with each person. The easier availability, the opportunity to receive time and touch, and the acknowledgment of inner needs found in the alternative high street clinics are all likely to result in an increase in the problem of dependence. In most cases the practitioners of alternative treatments, and indeed those involved in the healing ministry of Jesus, do not intend to become agents of ungodly control in our lives but we need to be very careful where we have placed our trust.

As Christians we are encouraged to be dependent on the Lord only. We praise Him for the knowledge and expertise He has given to those medical people who help treat our sicknesses, but we must not be wrongly dependent on them, or they will in effect become as gods to us. The source of all our healing and wholeness remains in God alone.

> *Do not let your hearts be troubled. Trust in God ...*
>
> (John 14:1 NIV)

It's good to ask questions!

Maybe this book has left you with lots of questions! We would encourage you to be good Bereans (Acts 17:10–11) and search the Scriptures, under the guidance of the Holy Spirit, for your own assessment of the validity of all that we have shared. Here are just a few questions from recent Ellel Ministries teaching courses on this subject, to which we've sought to give an answer:

Q: How can I protect a young person who is severely mentally ill and lives in a nursing home that is influenced by the teaching of Rudolph Steiner?

A: Our intercession, on behalf of those who are unable to fully understand or deal with spiritual danger for themselves, will always be valuable. We may not carry a direct responsibility for being able to change someone else's circumstances, but God looks for those willing to agree with Him about the defilement of this world through sin, and the effectiveness of His forgiveness and grace. We suggest that you forgive anyone who is promoting false spiritual comfort and ask for the Lord's protection for the person in need.

Q: Our son has suffered from epilepsy since the age of ten. He was practicing judo at the time. Could this have a link? We were not Christians then.

A: It is always worth asking the Lord. Martial arts are essentially a procedure designed to bring the body under a regime of physical and spiritual control in order to empower a person to overcome a combatant. This can bring inner disorder. There could also be wrong soul ties with the instructors and with the spiritual powers behind the art of judo and its root, ju-jitsu.

Q: I was told that it's OK to take homeopathic medicine up to the potency of 6c. Is this correct or shouldn't we take any homeopathic medicine?

A: It's interesting to use the word "potency." Where does the potency or power to "heal" come from? In homeopathy, the "strength" of the medication is said to increase as the dilution (defined by the "c" number) increases. There is no scientific basis for this increase of potency. If the solution does indeed contain any power, whatever the level of dilution, this power is from an unknown source and this should cause concern for any Christian.

Q: *If someone says they use alternative medicine because they prayed and God showed them to do it, what can I say?*

A: In the end, every decision we take in life either agrees or disagrees with God. If a person genuinely believes that God has directed them in the use of a particular remedy, then they must be free to make their own decision. Those around can only give whatever advice they feel best helps the one making the decision. We must never seek to control others through manipulation or intimidation. However, it could be useful to point them to relevant passages of Scripture that might help them to review the choice that they've made.

Q: *Many movies have martial arts in them. Does it influence us if we watch them? What about movies and TV in general?*

A: Our spiritual vulnerability throughout our lives depends on many things, such as the spiritual legacy from our forebears and the wounding and sinfulness of our own lives. No two people will be affected the same, but TV and cinema can certainly be an opportunity for the enemy to defile our lives, especially if we are actively looking for a place of escape or comfort from life's difficulties. It's best to see God as the solution.

Q: *Iridology surely isn't fortune-telling. It is used to see health in the body. I had my eyes done in England many years ago and the doctor said the blood vessels of my eyes showed I was angry. God used that to show me anger turned in against myself. How can that be evil?*

A: Of course our eyes can indeed show symptoms of disorder in the body. However, iridology takes this issue well beyond just recognizing the biological interrelationship between the eyes and the rest of the body. This diagnostic method is clearly based on an occult belief similar to the meridian pathways of reflexology.

Q: Could you explain the connection between Gnosticism and psychology?

A: Carl Jung was a famous Swiss psychiatrist deeply involved in the occult, including the use of spirit guides. Jungian psychology advocated the seeking of inner personal harmony through spiritual exploration and experience in practices such as kundalini yoga. Carl Jung's beliefs are sometimes described as a being a modern form of Gnosticism, a name given to a group of ancient beliefs in man's ability to understand the divine realms through mystical investigation and knowledge.

Q: Is there anything wrong with herbal teas to soothe the stomach? Are they like homeopathic remedies?

A: No. Normal herbal teas can be safely enjoyed for their refreshing aroma and flavor, as well as having chemical qualities that can be beneficial to the body. Just be cautious that the description of the product is not implying the transfer of any spiritual energy from the plants being used.

The answer is always Jesus

In this chapter we have suggested that the best way to avoid the dangers of spiritual deception through alternative treatments for sickness is to seek to live a godly and holy life. The closer we walk with Jesus, the more obvious the works of the enemy will be, and the less influence the powers of darkness can have in our lives. As part of the Body of Christ, we should aim to be in rightful relationship with one another, particularly with those called to be leaders and pastors among us. It is part of the responsibility of leadership to seek protection for the church community they lead.

The issue of authority in our lives needs to be looked at. When going into any form of medical treatment, we need to be sure under whose authority we rest – is it God's or the enemy's?

Prayer is the foundation of all healing for believers. Ask God for guidance in how best to treat the physical symptoms of ill health, while at the same time seeking Him for the deeper wholeness and freedom that He wants for our lives.

We need to live in reality rather than spiritual or emotional deception. Sickness resulting from our actions or those of others needs to be faced for what it is, and enemy attack needs to be discerned and dealt with appropriately. We have an amazing number of wonderful and powerful medical treatments these days, but it is always best to seek the ultimate wisdom of God.

Finally ...

Jesus made it clear that He came to bind up the broken-hearted and to set captives free (Luke 4:18). There is a pathway of restoration which God has prepared for all those who choose to trust Him. He knows exactly what is right and when it is right for each one of us, in this process. However, there is an enemy who seeks to steal God's true healing. Jesus calls him a murderer and a liar. We should be on our guard against this robber, especially when we feel a bit desperate for healing. The seductive offers of the powers of darkness may seem to provide supernatural help, but the spiritual side effects may bring more harm than help.

The best policy is to always talk to God about any new therapy that we are intending to try. He will alert us to the truth of what is on offer. In the appendix which follows, we have attempted to list some of the more common treatments and therapies which are available these days. It will never be possible to make a complete list, but the intention is to give guidelines for what to watch out for. It is very likely that some people will disagree with the comments that we have made. Our intention is simply to make Christians aware of some of the spiritual issues that can accompany so many of the remedies being promoted today. The practitioners are usually well intentioned and certainly intending no harm to patients, but a good intention does not guard against ignorance of the spiritual issues involved.

The authors' desire in writing this book has not been to promote fear or hostility towards alternative treatments and therapists, but to raise awareness of the fact that, when we seek healing on a pathway where there is unseen spiritual power, it is very important to know who is in control.

We believe Jesus is the safest Way.

A Summary of Some Treatments and Therapies which Could Have Spiritually Harmful Side Effects

Absent healing: A term frequently associated with reiki and referring to spiritual healing at a distance.

Acupressure: Similar to acupuncture but involving massage or pressure points throughout the body rather than the use of needles.

Acupuncture: Inserting needles at specific locations throughout the body in the belief that these will manipulate spiritual pathways and restore balance and health to the patient. Also used for anesthesia.

Applied kinesiology: A diagnostic technique (for disorders such as allergies) supposedly to ascertain energy imbalance in the body by measuring the physical resistance of certain muscles.

Aromatherapy: Medication, both internal and external, derived from the essential oils of plants, based on the belief that healing energy can be transferred from the plant to the body.

Auric healing: Diagnostic and healing techniques based on the belief that there are energy fields within and around the body (auras), which can be assessed and manipulated.

Bach flower remedies: Medication, usually internal, derived from plant material in a very weak solution of water and alcohol, based on a belief that certain flowers contain healing energy.

Bioenergy healing: A range of techniques, frequently using the hands of the therapist, apparently to assess and unblock the energy levels and pathways in and around the body.

Biomagnetic therapy: A practice developed by a doctor of acupuncture, using magnets placed on the body. There are strong links with practices such as meridian therapy and homeopathy.

Buqi healing: A non-touch healing technique using the hands to manipulate apparent negative energy in the body. Roots in qigong.

Chakra healing: Diagnostic and healing techniques based on a Hindu belief in the need to manipulate supposed energy centers in the body, particularly in the spine.

Chi healing: Diagnostic and healing techniques based on a Taoist belief in the need to balance the opposing spiritual forces of *yin* and *yang* within the body, in order to permit free flow of the universal life force, *chi*.

Chinese herbal medicine: Medication based on plants and animal parts, traditionally formulated in the belief that this will restore the harmony of the opposing spiritual forces within the body.

Chiropractic: Manipulation of the spine to deal with misalignments which are supposedly causing bodily dysfunction. The founder based the therapy on mystical principles of energy pathways. Most modern practitioners see the therapy as releasing nerve constriction.

Color therapy: The use of color and light to diagnose and apparently treat emotional and spiritual imbalance in the body. Frequently associated with *chakras*.

Cranial osteopathy: One of the more esoteric branches of osteopathy using head massage to apparently treat dysfunctional energy rhythms in the plates that make up the human skull.

Cranial-sacral therapy: Head massage intended to identify and release energy blockages.

Crystal therapy: Diagnostic and healing techniques using the supposed energy of small stones or crystals, placed on the body, to restore holistic balance and health.

Detox: Dietary procedures to apparently rid the body of all the unwanted toxins, despite the fact that the body has been designed to normally do this very effectively on its own

Dianetics: Diagnostic technique used in Scientology, apparently to determine mental dysfunction associated with spiritual identity.

Dowsing: Diagnostic techniques using various methods and instruments of divination.

Eurhythmy: Movement therapy developed by Rudolf Steiner supposedly able to enhance physical and spiritual development within the body.

Feng shui: Lifestyle belief in the physical positioning of possessions and property to supposedly align with geographical spiritual powers.

Homeopathy: Medication, usually internal, derived from plants in an extremely weak solution. It is believed that the dilution process empowers the medicine to bring healing.

Huna massage: A massage technique from Hawaii, believed to reunite the mind and the body with the spirit.

Hypnotherapy: Achieving an altered state of consciousness in order to bring the mind into a place of control, which will apparently have a positive effect on the dysfunction which is being treated.

Indian head massage: Technique from Hindu roots, to apparently unblock energy channels.

Iridology: Diagnostic technique in which the colors and patterns of the iris are believed to indicate the health of various organs of the body, through unseen connecting pathways.

Kirlian photography: A photographic technique apparently for diagnosing the condition of the aura, the supposed energy field around the body.

Kundalini awakening: A belief from Hindu roots in the existence of a spiritual energy center (*chakra*) at the base of the spine, regarded as a coiled snake which needs to be awakened and raised to a place of unity with the universal spirit. Strongly linked to yoga.

Martial arts: Mostly associated with practices from Asia, these are combative techniques intended to bring the body into a heightened place of physical and spiritual control.

Meditation: Many forms of mind concentration, using special body postures, mantras (word or sound repetition), breathing techniques, music, and visual objects. Releasing the mind into a place of emptiness or mystical control can open a door to the spiritual realm.

Mora Therapy™: Use of electronic equipment, apparently to measure and then cancel out the unbalanced energy patterns in the body which cause disorder.

Naturopathy: Healing practices that seek to minimize the use of prescription drugs and surgery. This covers a wide range of alternative therapies and medication. The founder saw the needs of the human body in spiritual terms.

Neuro-skeletal realignment: A massage therapy predominantly intended to release constraints in the central nervous system but also acknowledging the apparent significance of meridians, and often associated with acupuncture.

New Age healing: The New Age movement is an international network of groups and individuals exploring religious and philosophical ideas, in a quest for spiritual knowledge, enlightenment, and improvement. It embraces many alternative ways of healing.

Osteopathy (and osteopathic medicine): A massage therapy usually confined to dealing with musculoskeletal problems in the neck and spine, intended to improve the movement of body fluids. Controversially, some practitioners operate out of a strongly holistic approach which seeks to bring balance to the interconnections between the organs and structures of the body.

Pilates: Exercise routines believed by the founder to be a way of bringing well-being to the body through physical and spiritual control.

Qigong (chi kung): This is similar to tai chi but is not a martial art. It is an internal meditation technique using certain postures and breathing techniques to improve the flow of the supposed life force *qi* (*chi*) through the body.

Radiesthesia: The detection of apparent spiritual radiation or aura around the body, using dowsing or divination instruments such as rods or a pendulum held over the client.

Radionics: Diagnostic technique using devices to measure the apparent frequency of the body's energy output.

Reflexology: Massage of specific parts of the sole of the feet in the belief that these are linked by spiritual pathways to the various organs of the body.

Reiki: Spiritual healing using the palms of the practitioner as a channel of supposed universal healing energy. Practitioners seek to progress to the master or teacher degree of ability.

Shiatsu: A diagnostic and healing massage therapy from Japan, incorporating beliefs similar to those associated with acupressure.

Somatic movement training: A range of movement and breathing exercises intended to enhance physical and emotional well-being. Sometimes linked to yoga.

Tai chi (chuan): Martial art believed to bring spiritual balance and health to the body by slow meditative movements. Based on the principles of *yin* and *yang*.

Thai massage: Massage and stretching of the *sen* pathways (similar to meridians) in the body, supposedly to improve spiritual flow and health.

Transcendental Meditation: A technique for apparently attaining spiritual harmony and enlightenment, based on Hindu beliefs.

Tuina massage: A massage technique, often used along with acupuncture, to apparently restore spiritual balance to the body.

Yoga: A practice intended to progressively bring a person into spiritual unity with a supreme deity of Hinduism, through a series of steps involving meditation, breathing exercises, and bodily postures.

Zero balancing: Specific massaging and stretching procedures to apparently bring the body's energy back into balance. Roots in acupuncture.

About Ellel Ministries

Our Vision

Ellel Ministries is a non-denominational Christian Mission Organization with a vision to resource and equip the Church by welcoming people, teaching them about the Kingdom of God and healing those in need (Luke 9:11).

Our Mission

Our mission is to fulfill the above vision throughout the world, as God opens the doors, in accordance with the Great Commission of Jesus and the calling of the Church to proclaim the Kingdom of God by preaching the good news, healing the broken-hearted and setting the captives free. We are, therefore, committed to evangelism, healing, deliverance, discipleship and training. The particular scriptures on which our mission is founded are Isaiah 61:1–7; Matthew 28:18–20; Luke 9:1–2; 9:11; Ephesians 4:12; 2 Timothy 2:2.

Our Basis of Faith

God is a Trinity. God the Father loves all people. God the Son, Jesus Christ, is Savior and Healer, Lord and King. God the Holy Spirit indwells Christians and imparts the dynamic power by which they are enabled to continue Christ's ministry. The Bible is the divinely inspired authority in matters of faith, doctrine and conduct, and is the basis for teaching.

For more information

Please visit our website at www.ellelministries.org for full up-to-date information about the world-wide work of Ellel Ministries.

Ellel Ministries Centers

International Headquarters

Ellel Grange
Ellel, Lancaster LA2 0HN, UK
t: +44 (0) 1524 751651
f: +44 (0) 1524 751738
e: info.grange@ellelministries.org

Ellel Glyndley Manor
Stone Cross, Pevensey, E. Sussex
BN24 5BS, UK
t: +44 (0) 1323 440440
f: +44 (0) 1323 440877
e: info.glyndley@ellelministries.org

Ellel Pierrepont
Frensham, Farnham, Surrey
GU10 3DL, UK
t: +44 (0) 1252 794060
f: +44 (0) 1252 794039
e: info.pierrepont@ellelministries.org

Ellel Scotland
Blairmore House, Glass, Huntly,
Aberdeenshire AB54 4XH, Scotland
t: +44 (0) 1466 799102
f: +44 (0) 1466 700205
e: info.scotland@ellelministries.org

Ellel Ministries Northern Ireland
240 Rashee Road, Ballyclare, County
Antrim, BT39 9JQ, Northern Ireland
t: +44 (0) 28 9334 4401
e: info.northernireland@ellelministries.org

Ellel Ministries Africa
PO Box 39569, Faerie Glen 0043, Pretoria,
South Africa
t: +27 (0) 12 809 0031/1172
f: +27 12 809 1173
e: info.africa@ellelministries.org

Ellel Ministries Australia (Sydney)
Gilbulla, 710 Moreton Park Road,
Menangle, 2568, NSW, Australia
t: +61 (02) 4633 8102
f: +61 (02) 4633 8201
e: info.gilbulla@ellelministries.org

Ellel Ministries Australia Headquarters (Perth)
Springhill, PO Box 609, Northam, WA, 6401, Australia
t: +61 (08) 9622 5568
f: +61 (08) 9622 5123
e: info.springhill@ellelministries.org

Ellel Ministries Canada
Derbyshire Downs
183 Hanna Rd., RR#2, Westport, Ontario, K0G 1X0, Canada
t: +1 (613) 273 8700
e: info.ontario@ellelministries.org

Ellel Ministries Canada West
10-5918 5 St SE, Calgary, Alberta, T2H 1L4, Canada
t: +1 (403) 238 2008
f: +1 (866) 246 5918
e: info.calgary@ellelministries.org

Ellel Ministries France
(Fraternité Chrétienne)
10 Avenue Jules Ferry, 38380 Saint Laurent du Pont, France
t: +33 (0)4 56 99 42 663
e: info.france@ellelministries.org

Ellel Ministries Germany
Bahnhoffstr. 43-47, 72213 Altensteig, Deutschland
w: http://www.ellelgermany.de
t: +49 (0) 7453 275 51
e: info.germany@ellelministries.org

Ellel Ministries Hungary
Veresegyház, PF17, 2112, Hungary
t/f: +36 28 362396
e: info.hungary@ellelministries.org

Ellel East Regional Nations
Veresegyház, PF17, 2112, Hungary
t: +36 28 362410
f: +36 28 362396
e: info.regionalnations@ellelministries.org

Ellel India
502, Orchid, Holy Cross Road, IC Colony, Borivli West, Mumbai 400 103, India
mobile: +91 (0) 93 2224 5209
e: info.india@ellelministries.org

Ellel Ministries Malaysia
Lot 2, Ground and 1st Floor, Wisma Leven Lorong Margosa 2, Luyang Phase 8, 88300 Kota Kinabalu, Sabah, Malaysia
t: +6088 270246
f: +6088 270280
e: info.malaysia@ellelministries.org

Ellel Ministries Netherlands
Wichmondseweg 19, 7223 LH Baak, Netherlands
t: +31 575 441452
e: info.netherlands@ellelministries.org

Ellel Ministries New Zealand
info.newzealand@ellelministries.org

Ellel Ministries Norway
Stiftelsen Ellel Ministries Norge, Hogstveien 2, 2006 Løvenstad, Norge (Norway)
t: +47 67413150
e: info.norway@ellelministries.org

Ellel Ministries Singapore
Thomson Post Office, PO Box 204, Singapore 915707
t: +65 6252 4234
f: +65 6252 3792
e: info.singapore@ellelministries.org

Ellel Ministries Sweden
Kvarnbackavägen 4 B, 711 92 Vedevåg, Sweden
t: +46 581 93140
e: info.sweden@ellelministries.org

Ellel Ministries USA
1708 English Acres Drive, Lithia, Florida, 33547, USA
t: +1 (813) 737 4848
f: +1 (813) 737 9051
e: info.usa@ellelministries.org

*All details are correct at time of going to press (September 2010) but are subject to change.

About the Authors

David Cross

David Cross is the regional director for Ellel Ministries in Western Europe. He is based at Ellel Glyndley Manor near Eastbourne, UK. He qualified as a civil engineer but developed many life skills in a most varied working career, which included leading ski tours in the Scottish Highlands. Despite fulfillment at work, David found himself gradually more and more disillusioned with the ethos of "self-sufficiency" on which he had based his life up until that point. A change in direction came when he was converted in Hong Kong in the early 1980s and he eagerly began to follow Jesus. On returning to the UK in 1984 he became an elder in the Church of Scotland. Then in 1993, he and his wife Denise joined Ellel Ministries. David's clear and authoritative teaching from God's Word has brought understanding and healing to many who have been confused and damaged by the ideologies of today's world. David has written three other books in the Truth & Freedom series published by Sovereign World: *Soul Ties: The Unseen Bond in Relationships, God's Covering: A Place of Healing*, and *Trapped by Control: How to Find Freedom*.

John Berry

Born in 1949 into a Christian family, John's father was a Baptist minister. John was himself an accredited Baptist minister for thirty-three years, and before that was involved in running a group of building companies. He has been married for almost thirty-nine years to Jennie and has two children and six grandchildren. John and his wife were called to Ellel Ministries Glyndley Manor near Eastbourne three years ago as wardens and team pastors. Amongst his various roles, John also works as a modular school manager, is a teacher, and is also a member of the Leadership Support Group.

Other titles in the Truth & Freedom Series

Also available in eBook format from all the major eBook retailers

Anger
How do you handle it?
Paul & Liz Griffin
RRP: £6.99
Size: 5.5"x8.5"
Pages: 112
ISBN: 9781852404505

Hope & Healing for the
Abused
Paul & Liz Griffin
RRP: £7.99
Size: 5.5"x8.5"
Pages: 128
ISBN: 9781852404802

Intercession & Healing
Breaking through with God
Fiona Horrobin
RRP: £7.99
Size: 5.5"x8.5"
Pages: 176
ISBN: 9781852405007

Soul Ties
The unseen bond in
relationships
David Cross
RRP: £7.99
Size: 5.5"x8.5"
Pages: 128
ISBN: 9781852404512

God's Covering
A place of healing
David Cross
RRP: £8.99
Size: 5.5"x8.5"
Pages: 192
ISBN: 9781852404857

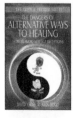

The Dangers of Alternative
Ways to Healing
How to avoid new age
deceptions
David Cross & John Berry
RRP: £8.99
Size: 5.5"x8.5"
Pages: 176
ISBN: 9781852405373

Trapped by Control
How to find freedom
David Cross
RRP: £7.99
Size: 5.5"x8.5"
Pages: 112
ISBN: 9781852405014

Rescue from Rejection
Finding Security in God's
Loving Acceptance
Denise Cross
RRP: £7.99
Size: 5.5"x8.5"
Pages: 160
ISBN: 9781852405380

Sex, God's Truth
Jill Southern
RRP: £7.99
Size: 5.5"x8.5"
Pages: 128
ISBN: 9781852404529

Stepping Stones to the
Father Heart of God
Margaret Silvester
RRP: £8.99
Size: 5.5" x 8.5"
Pages: 176
ISBN: 9781852406233

www.sovereignworld.com

We hope you enjoyed reading this Sovereign World book. For more details of other Sovereign books and new releases see our website:

www.sovereignworld.com

You can also join us on Facebook and Twitter.

To promote this title kindly consider writing a review on our Facebook page or for posting to an online retailer.

If you would like to help us send a copy of this book and many other titles to needy pastors in developing countries, please write for further information or send your gift to:

Sovereign World Trust
PO Box 777, Tonbridge, Kent, TN11 0ZS
United Kingdom

www.sovereignworldtrust.com

The Sovereign World Trust is a registered charity.

Lightning Source UK Ltd.
Milton Keynes UK
UKOW06f0804310816

281837UK00001B/60/P